Building A Libr

A Listener's Guide

ᴏ

by arrangement with th̲ ̲British Broadcasting Corporation

Edited by JOHN LADE

London

OXFORD UNIVERSITY PRESS

New York   Melbourne

1979

Oxford University Press, Walton Street, Oxford OX2 6DP

OXFORD LONDON GLASGOW NEW YORK
TORONTO MELBOURNE WELLINGTON
IBADAN NAIROBI DAR ES SALAAM CAPE TOWN
KUALA LUMPUR SINGAPORE JAKARTA HONG KONG TOKYO
DELHI BOMBAY CALCUTTA MADRAS KARACHI

ISBN 0 19 311324 4

*Printed and bound in Great Britain by
Ebenezer Baylis and Son Limited,
The Trinity Press, Worcester, and London*

Contents

Contents

Preface

JOHN LADE

'Building a Library', as Saturday morning listeners to BBC Radio Three will know, has been a regular feature of *Record Review*, a programme for record enthusiasts I have edited and introduced since 1957. I was a producer in the BBC's Gramophone Department when plans were laid for the programme, and although from time to time we have made slight modifications to its form and content our main objectives have always been to review new records and also to help listeners who wanted to build up a basic collection. 'Building a *Library*' has never seemed to be the ideal definition of what we were about, but we have yet to find a better word: 'Discorama' lacked dignity and 'Building a Discothèque' would have had other connotations! We decided that each week in this part of *Record Review* all the currently available versions of an important work would be compared by a critic who was an authority on the particular composer or style of music under review and who, without being excessively academic, would be able to communicate enthusiasm and justify a preference for certain performances rather than others.

We were aware in those early days, just as we are today, that as more and more recordings of a work are issued it becomes increasingly difficult (often quite impossible) to hear every version in the shops. Our critics do listen to *all* the available records of the work they are considering (though perhaps weeding out a few before coming to the studio) and can illustrate the points they make with excerpts from any performances they choose. The selection of works to be reviewed depends on many things: requests from listeners, new issues of special interest likely to alter previous recommendations, and, of course, the possibility of considering works that have not previously been the subject of a comparative review or for which a reappraisal has long been overdue. The collection of reviews printed here offers a permanent record of roughly one season's programmes and it shows, I think, the wide range of music we cover, including as it does Bach's Sonatas and Partitas for solo violin, Schumann's *Liederkreis* Op. 39, Wagner's *Tristan und Isolde*, Schoenberg's *Pierrot Lunaire*, and Prokofiev's Third Piano Concerto. We also include from time to time a guide to the recorded repertory of certain composers who, however distinguished they may be, have no single work available in a sufficient number of recordings to make a comparative review a practical possibility. The music of Frank Bridge, of which a survey is included here, is a case in point.

Each review in this collection is supplemented by a complete list of recordings discussed, together with their numbers. In the main, the recordings are arranged in chronological order according to date of issue, the reviewers' recommendations being marked with an asterisk; for the three articles on composers, however, the recordings are listed in alphabetical order according to title. Every effort has been made to keep the reviews up to date since the time of the broadcasts, and to see that all the numbers are accurate at the time of going to press. For example, a record which was once at full price may reappear at medium price with a new number. In fact many things can happen in the gramophone world between proof stage and final publication of a book of this kind. Records we have considered may be deleted (though there may still be odd copies in some shops), new versions may appear, and existing ones may cease to be available singly but only as part of a boxed set. These are just some of the things that make life difficult for editors and reviewers, as well as record collectors.

I have had to take certain editorial liberties in making scripts read in what I hope is an easily comprehensible style without the musical examples so important in the broadcasts. In achieving this I have to thank all the contributors and the staff of the Oxford University Press for their patience and helpful suggestions, and the BBC for giving the project its blessing.

To the memory of
Anna Instone
(1912–1978)

Bizet   *Carmen*

RODNEY MILNES

I must say straight away that *Carmen* was already one of my desert-island operas; intensive listening has increased my admiration for it a hundred-fold, something I should not have thought possible. The subtlety of the music and the interplay of the characters is simply immeasurable. Two points first. It is odd that in eight recordings of one of France's great dramatic masterpieces there should not be a single French singer of Carmen or Don José, and to give you a clue as to which way my mind is running, the two best Carmens are Spanish, which is not inappropriate, and the two best Josés are both Russo-Swedish in the single person of Nicolai Gedda. Second, the important problem of text. There is what used to be the standard version with recitatives by Guiraud, and the original version with spoken dialogue that finds more favour today. But it is not as easy as that: no two of the available recordings use exactly the same text. I have to say I infinitely prefer the dialogue version: that is what Bizet wrote, and it is perfectly, and classically, structured; the recitatives take longer to tell you less about the characters, and they are bad recitatives anyway. Still, many people first got to know *Carmen* that way, and the Guiraud recordings must be considered. The sets split down the middle chronologically: four Guiraud, followed by four with varying amounts of dialogue.

One of the early recitative recordings is on Decca: it has a bright, clear, forward sound characteristic of its time, which was 1963; the fashion nowadays is for more recessed and spacious sound, and it is a fashion that I hope will pass. This set has a vivid production by John Culshaw with lots of rhubarb and foot-stamping, a chorus and orchestra from Geneva that sound idiomatic under Thomas Schippers's direction, and a good, raucous children's chorus. But that is about it. Mario Del Monaco is a wholly unacceptable José, way outside his *Fach*, and Joan Sutherland is a dull Micaela. Regina Resnik is an exciting singer on stage, but the excitement fails to transfer to records; her plummy, rather monochrome voice tends to spread and become raw under pressure, so this version is not really in the running. The following year came two recitative recordings, one on RCA with Karajan and forces from Vienna. This too is vividly produced by Culshaw, but Karajan's speeds might be called leisurely when they work, and far too slow when they do not, which is rather more often than not; and this very French, piquant score tends to drag. He over-realizes the expression to a fault, and makes Micaela's music sound sentimental, which is a great crime in my book. He also makes very heavy weather of the recitatives, and the final effect is heavy, mannered, and unidiomatic. His Carmen is Leontyne Price, and her smoky, slightly husky tone is ideally suited to at least one aspect of the roll. In the Seguidille, for instance, she is as *pianissimo* as possible, as marked by Bizet, and I like the humorous quality of her singing. Elsewhere, though, she veers towards a heavier, dramatic reading, to some extent governed by Karajan's approach. The José in this version is Franco Corelli, and he poses the eternal problem of this role: his heroic delivery makes for much excitement in the later acts, but he cannot summon the delicacy of tone or phrase required for the first act and the Flower Song, and his French is very poor. Together, he and Price make much of the Finale, but with Karajan worrying the music it does sound a bit too much like Puccini or Mascagni, and not quite enough like Bizet. The Vienna Philharmonic is of course good, and so is the chorus, though the ladies sound more like waitresses from Café Demel than workers in a cigarette factory in Seville, and the Vienna Boys' Choir is impossibly respectable.

In the same year, 1964, came what was known as the 'Callas Carmen', and that is what it is. It is a special case, and Callas fans will want to have it. Characteristic of Callas, to take the Habanera as an example, is her colouring of the words, with special emphasis on 'jamais': love has 'never' known any rules. But for all the verbal interest, there is nothing remotely beautiful about her singing anywhere on these records, and this slides over into her characterization. Her Carmen is a forceful, elemental, ultimately unsympathetic character, and one who is really beastly to José in the last act. I do not believe this is what Bizet intended: indeed, she is nearer to Mérimée's Carmen than Bizet's. Georges Prêtre, the only French conductor on these eight sets, at least makes something of the Guiraud recitatives by zipping through them at top speed, but, conversely, his is perhaps too Gallic and light-weight a reading, though it does have some elegance. The smaller roles and of course chorus and orchestra are all French, which is a plus, and the Micaela, Andrea Guiot, is the most French and lively of them all, though her voice is by no means pretty. No, the main attraction of this set is Gedda's José, as he is the one singer who has the technique to cope with all aspects of this incredibly difficult role. On no other recording is the Flower Song sung exactly as Bizet wrote it, or with such delicacy as that with which Gedda sings that treacherous penultimate phrase, where most tenors bellow the *pianissimo* B flat.

I find Gedda's José even better on the earliest of these sets, the one conducted by Beecham and released in 1960, though it does not in the least sound its age. Admittedly Sir Thomas's slow speed for the Flower Song makes it much more difficult for Gedda to match the singing of his later version, but taken as a whole I think this is the best José on LP. A lot of Beecham's speeds are slow, but unlike Karajan he sustains them convincingly rather than over-pointing once he has set them. This is a wonderfully idiomatic and satisfying reading with, again, largely French forces. The Carmen is Victoria de los Angeles, and I think she is still the best of all. In the Habanera I love her humour, her teasing colouring of the words, and her luscious portamentos; and Beecham allows just enough flexibility within the basic tempo. This is singing and vocal characterization of the very highest order. And the character develops, too, attaining a truly tragic dimension in the last act, countering her lover's jealousy with dignity and reasonableness, and, although de los Angeles is a soprano, she can, when required, more than deliver the mezzo range. Her Carmen is sung with stunning force and Gedda is at his most anguished in this set, which has good supporting singers and a fair chorus and orchestra. I have not said anything about Escamillos yet, as it is a role in which it is hard to fail or wholly to succeed, and Ernest Blanc is one of the best. Janine Micheau's Micaela is authoritative, and ideal in all but her slightly maternal tone, which again is not wholly inappropriate. Beecham also gives full emotional weight to Micaela's music without ever sentimentalizing it, and I think this is very important. I should also add that there is a snatch of dialogue in this recitative version that does not appear in the latest two recordings: the lines at the first meeting of Carmen and José, when he tells her he is making a chain for his priming pin, a line that I hope Freud never heard. This Beecham set is clearly the best of the recitative versions, and as it is at medium price it must be one of my recommendations.

The first of the four dialogue versions came in 1970, and is something of a rogue elephant among the eight, as it reconstructs what is thought to have been played on the first night, or rather what is printed in the 1875 vocal score which was published under Bizet's supervision. Thus we have the Pantomime for Morales and the chorus in the first act, which Bizet cut during the original run and which cannot be heard on any other recording, and the full version of the Duel Duet, which we can and should hear elsewhere. Although this HMV set is of great interest to *Carmen* specialists, it has some serious drawbacks. The dialogue is delivered by actors whose voices do not begin to match those of the singers, thus destroying any sense of a performance. Frühbeck de Burgos's conducting is strangely stodgy, and so, even more strangely, is Grace Bumbry's Carmen, She is another of those exciting stage personalities seldom heard to best advantage on record. The José is Jon Vickers, and his intensity of emotion certainly comes across, but his quest for expressiveness leads to his approaching notes from underneath too often, which gives an odd, bleating sort of feel to his singing, in general, and scuppers his otherwise praise-worthy attempt at the Flower Song. Also on this set there is a good, swaggering Escamillo from Kostas Paskalis, and Mirella Freni's second Micaela (her first was for Karajan). Of course she sings beautifully, but I find her reading too meek and submissive. A flawed recording, then, but with an interesting text for Bizet enthusiasts.

The three remaining sets either use, or use parts of, the Oeser edition which is, to put it very mildly, controversial. It not only restores some of the cuts made by Bizet, but in one or two vital places prints seriously wrong readings. As to the cuts, I think Bizet was right to make them in theatrical terms, though it is nice to hear as much of his music as possible on record. The first set, on Deutsche Grammophon, is based on the Metropolitan Opera production and conducted by Leonard Bernstein, and it could be dismissed straight off but for one factor. Everything I said about Karajan's conducting applies here, but cubed. Bernstein does some most peculiar things to the score (Oeser's, by the way) but with a version of the Duel Duet that would have Bizet spinning in his grave: he adopts slow tempos that really do not work, and over-points the expression to a wholly harmful extent. This is the sort of conducting that draws attention to itself rather than to the composer and I think words had better fail me. James McCracken is the José: he is pretty faithful to the markings, but his tone is too quavery for the role. The supporting cast is fair, and they speak the dialogue in a bewildering variety of French accents. The one positive factor is Marilyn Horne in the title-role. She has an ideal Carmen voice and could be outstanding with a more helpful conductor.

And so to the two most recent and best dialogue sets, from Solti on Decca and Abbado on Deutsche Grammophon. The choice is really impossible. If it were just a matter of the title-role then Abbado would win hands down, for his Carmen is Teresa Berganza; marvellous in the Seguidille is the way she points the marcatos and the mixture of humour and seductiveness with which she uses the words, and she sustains the same level of musicianship and vivid characterization throughout. Her Card Song is the best of any on LP. The José is common to both these recordings: Placido Domingo. Like so many others, he is very effective in the later, heavier acts, but has difficulties with the Micaela duet and either cannot, or will not, sing the end of the Flower Song *pianissimo*. He is at his best in the Finale, and this is where Berganza is tested too, but not beyond her limits. The Deutsche Grammophon sound is clearer than Decca's but occasionally a little shallow. Abbado's conducting is consistently exciting, alert, fleet, and dramatic, possibly at times a little brash. Solti may lack the same degree of Mediterranean brilliance, but he does supply some of the depth of feeling not always found with Abbado. I must repeat that, if it were just Carmen, then Deutsche Grammophon is the clear choice, because, although Decca's Tatiana Troyanos has a nicely sensuous Carmen voice and is a sound performer, she cannot match her Spanish colleague's lively reading. But there are other characters. I feel very strongly that Micaela is not just an aberration on the part of the librettists, but an important and potentially heroic figure, and Decca has to my mind the better exponent of the role in Kiri Te Kanawa. Her tone is full and creamy, and she is meticulous in her attention to the markings; and, like Beecham, Solti lends full emotional weight to the Micaela/José duet in Act 1.

Te Kanawa's singing, then, is matchless, but Abbado also has a good Micaela in Ileana Cotrubas. She sings most sensitively, but her sweet vibrato accentuates the meekness of her characterization, rather like Freni's Decca has the more idiomatic and colourful Escamillo in José van Dam: Deutsche Grammophon's Sherrill Milnes is good, no more. There is little to choose between the playing of the London Symphony Orchestra on Deutsche Grammophon and the London Philharmonic Orchestra on Decca: the former is clearer, the latter more full-bodied. The smaller roles are much more strongly cast on Decca, with good French smugglers, and a lovely Mercedes from Jane Berbié. The dialogue, too, is fuller on Decca and more imaginatively delivered: this is the one aspect in which Troyanos is preferable to Berganza. And the transition between dialogue and music is more cunningly managed by Decca's producer Christopher Raeburn, and it all flows very naturally. There are one or two nasty moments of Oeser and one bad cut on Deutsche Grammophon, whereas Decca took great trouble to arrive at the best possible text, as Solti explains in the booklet. To sum up, it is almost impossible; at medium price and with recitative, it is clearly Beecham. At full price, and if money is no object, have both Abbado and Solti; if it is, then I think it must be Solti by the merest whisker, as his is the more complete and considered reading of this complex masterpiece.

Recordings Discussed

*de los Angeles, Gedda, Micheau, Blanc/ Paris ORTF/Chorus/Beecham	HMV SLS 5021
Resnik, Del Monaco, Sutherland, Krause/ Suisse Romande Orchestra and Chorus/ Schippers	Decca SET 256–8
Price, Corelli, Merrill, Freni/Vienna Boys Choir/Vienna Philharmonic Chorus and Orchestra/Karajan	RCA SER 5600
Callas, Gedda, Massard, Guisot/Duclos Chorus/Paris Opera/Prêtre	HMV SLS 913
Bumbry, Vickers, Paskalis, Freni/Chorus/ Paris Opera/Frühbeck	HMV SLS 952
Horne, McCracken, Krause, Maliponte/ New York Metropolitan Opera/Bernstein	Deutsche Grammophon 2740 101
*Troyanos, Domingo, Te Kanawa, van Dam/Choir of Haberdashers' School, Elstree/Alldis Choir/London Philharmonic Orchestra/Solti	Decca D 11 D3
*Berganza, Domingo, Milnes, Cotrubas/ Scottish Opera Chorus/London Symphony Orchestra/Abbado	Deutsche Grammophon 2709 083

© Rodney Milnes

Puccini   *Madama Butterfly*

ALAN BLYTH

There are no less than eight versions of this opera to choose from, and on no occasion was the truism that the better is the enemy of the good more true. So even the reject level is quite high. Out goes the RCA version with Leontyne Price conducted by Leinsdorf because, in spite of the lovely sounds she makes, Miss Price's little-girl effects soon prove embarrassing. Out goes no less a diva than Montserrat Caballé. She is a not inconsiderable Cio-Cio-San, but her performance is surrounded by mediocrity on her Spanish-made Decca set. Out goes, with a good deal more regret, another Decca recording, this time with Renata Tebaldi in the title role. She, like Price, is unbelievable as the child-bride, although her full-throated and immensely secure singing has much to commend it as such, particularly in the opera's later stages. So does that of the Pinkerton, Carlo Bergonzi. Tullio Serafin is the expansive conductor. Tebaldi enthusiasts will want this performance, and will not be disappointed, except possibly in the recorded sound which, in the set's latest manifestation, is cramped.

Having dispensed with the services of three such prima donnas, I will certainly have to justify others to take their place. Renata Scotto, for one, has long been acknowledged as a formidable interpreter of the title-role. She has recorded the part twice. The older of her performances, with Sir John Barbirolli as conductor, has stood the test of time. Indeed there are few sets that survive as long as twelve years in the HMV catalogue without good reason. Its qualities, among them Scotto's well-judged yet spontaneous expression and Barbirolli's vibrant conducting of the Rome Opera Orchestra, are, for instance, apparent at the start of the second act, where Butterfly tells Suzuki that Pinkerton promised to return when the robins nested, and then insists to her doubting servant that he will return – tornera'.

Much later Scotto returned to the studios, this time for CBS and with Lorin Maazel as conductor to record Butterfly again. In this performance her singing is more refined and certain, and the control of dynamics and portamento more delicate. Throughout, her portrayal has gained in vocal finesse, but it has been brought at the expense of the natural spontaneity that informs her reading for Barbirolli. Indeed the conductors may play a part in this different definition of the role. Nobody has lavished so much technical control on the score as Maazel, nobody brought out more eagerly its twentieth-century leanings, ably supported by the Philharmonia Orchestra, but all this can sound self-conscious, especially when set beside Barbirolli's more intuitive, less detailed interpretation. The immediate HMV Rome acoustic, as compared with the more aseptic and distanced CBS recording, only adds to the marked contrast in these two sets. An even warmer sound than HMV's is captured on the 1975 Karajan version for Decca. Here, in partnership with the Vienna Philharmonic, he obtained the most luscious, lustrous *Butterfly* yet. It is also the most controversially slow, expansive, emotionally indulgent interpretation ever committed to disc. The success or otherwise of the Karajan approach – and whether you will appreciate its special qualities – is most apparent in the passage where Butterfly, having sighted the *Abraham Lincoln,* Pinkerton's ship, thinks that he has returned. The impact is overwhelming: Then Karajan follows it with an eccentrically slow Flower Duet. His Butterfly is Mirella Freni, a volatile yet vulnerable portrayal, sung with unfailingly lovely tone and instinctively fine phrasing. Freni has as her servant the sympathetic, but rather grand Suzuki of Christa Ludwig. When he first recorded *Butterfly*, twenty years earlier, in 1955, Karajan took a rather different and less exaggerated view of the music. And he would not have dared to drown the last note of his prima donna on the word 'M'ama', for she was no less a soprano than Maria Callas. Callas took the role on stage only once, at Chicago, but she leaves no doubt in her records that she has studied it with her usual thoroughness and understanding. Hardly a phrase passes without a Callas colouring or perception. Her voice can be fined down for the little-girl effects of Act 1, show sweetness in the Yamadori episode, and turn to tragic depth in the final scene. Her ability to fine down her tone to the needs of the role and then expand it to *spinto* proportions is nowhere better shown than in the first-act episode where Butterfly touchingly tells Pinkerton that she has resigned her native religion and become a Christian. This is all delicately told. Then at 'Amor mio' – the rising cry of love – she shows that at least for her this means for all time. Karajan, as is his way in both his sets, supports his singer with a long-phrased accompaniment.

We still have one more Cio-Cio-San – and a famous one at that – Victoria de los Angeles. She was the first Butterfly I ever saw or heard, at Covent Garden more than twenty years ago. I recall hers as an infinitely tender and moving portrayal but even then to my untutored ears there seemed some strain to the lyrical voice at climaxes, as if the role was just one league above her. But then and now there is no doubting the simplicity and innate musicality of her singing; the way you can almost see a particular emotion in her tone remains hers alone. She rends the heart in the second-act passage, 'Che tua madre', where Butterfly tells Consul Sharpless that she could not beg in the streets crying charity for an unhappy mother, nor take up a profession that would lead to dishonour. No, dying would be better. You will find the sound at this point is for the most part golden, and the expression almost palpable. Victoria de los Angeles's HMV version, recently reissued at mid-price, is idiomatically but not very individually conducted by Gabriele Santini. It has the advantage of Jussi Björling, no less, as Pinkerton. This was to be Björling's last complete opera recording, made in 1960, the year of his death. His virile account of the part, sung in glowing tones, shows no sign of vocal decline, but his interpretation is a generalized one, not suggesting the carefree pleasure-seeking of Act 1 nor the wholehearted remorse of Act 2.

As with the title-role, standards of singing in the role of Pinkerton are high in our five sets. Placido Domingo, for Scotto's second performance, is similar to Björling. The tone pours out with almost Caruso-like power and with plenty of passion, but this might be any one of the Puccini heroes Domingo enacts so involvingly. Carlo Bergonzi, in the Scotto/Barbirolli set, is more imaginative, singing with both character and fine ardour, inspired by the moment. In the Callas set we hear the young Nicolai Gedda and nobody floats the start of the Love Duet more airily than he, observing Puccini's *dolcissimo* and *piano* marks, irresistibly seductive; Callas, too, shows similar artistry. Freni's Pinkerton, in the second Karajan recording, is Luciano Pavarotti and he manages to display a kind of boyish charm and palpitating ardour in the first act not equalled by any other tenor. He shows this specially in the Love Duet, matching the beauty and intensity of Freni's singing. A glorious carpet of sound is here provided by Karajan and the Vienna Philharmonic. Bergonzi, as I have already mentioned, is the admirable Pinkerton on the Scotto/Barbirolli set and her Sharpless is still better. Indeed Rolando Panerai is unsurpassed in the role in any recording. His firm, characterful baritone has an attractive quick vibrato; his diction is as exemplary, as is Scotto's.

Barbirolli once said, 'The most difficult parts in *Butterfly* are those nobody ever notices', but he is more adept than any other conductor in bringing them off. Nobody could doubt the importance of the final scene. Here in the second part of Act 2 (Act 3 as it is sometimes called) Puccini's interpreters show their true mettle. By the severest standards, Maazel's version, Scotto's second, fails. She shows great conviction, but Maazel's comparative coolness and CBS's distanced and variable recording do not fulfil all the music's demands, though let me stress that in a less competitive field one could well be satisfied with this version. Nor does Santini match up to the score's requirements. I am reluctant to pass over de los Angeles's in many ways memorable portrayal, but she lacks the sustained intensity of tone needed for those searing last pages. I am now left with the two Karajan sets and the Barbirolli. In his later version, Karajan is at his most persuasive in the great trio for Suzuki, sung by Christa Ludwig, Pinkerton, the lamenting Pavarotti, and Sharpless, sung in this set with warmth and understanding by Robert Kerns. Pinkerton's aria of remorse is well sung by all the tenors, when Butterfly reappears, sees Kate Pinkerton, and finally is brought face to face with the truth, Callas is supreme. Not long before, she has marvellously enacted the moment of Cio-Cio-San's false dawn. Now, as she tells Kate that under the arches of heaven there is no happier woman than you – 'Sotto il gran ponte del cielo' – Callas's Butterfly pours out her whole soul and being.

Freni is almost as touching here, her tone more consistently even than Callas's. This is one of her best, if not *the* best, portrait she has drawn for the gramophone, imaginative and deeply felt. Yet, at this juncture, and many others, I do feel that Karajan stretches the tempos not only well beyond those suggested by the composer but beyond the needs of the music. Barbirolli, never a conductor precisely in a hurry himself, makes all the points without the dragging effect. Besides, Karajan, in this later version, often places the orchestra too much in the forefront of things, and exaggerates many of the dynamic effects. I do not want to make too much of either of these points, because while you are listening to his sumptuous Decca set on its own it is inclined to exert its seductive power—it certainly did so on me – but the result is closer to Richard Strauss than to Puccini. It is a set, if you can afford the luxury, to have as a second choice, for indulgent occasions. In his earlier, HMV recording, Karajan was much stricter with himself and the results are correspondingly tauter, more dramatic. The sound, in electronically processed stereo, is not as spacious as one might wish, yet the balance is often fairer to the voices than on his Decca version. And Karajan is here partnering a truly inspired Callas at the peak of her form, supported by Gedda's sensitive Pinkerton, Borriello's sympathetic Sharpless, and Lucia Danieli's actively engaged Suzuki. At mid-price, I consider the set a bargain.

But the central performance of *Madama Butterfly* for me, indeed one of the classics of the gramophone, comes from Sir John Barbirolli and his team. This is at once the most spontaneous, the most theatre-like reading, down to the occasional audible contribution from Sir John himself. Scotto, in the title role, is the most complete and involved Cio-Cio-San, one aware of every facet of the role and with the ability to convey in appropriate tone and verbal inflection, and in this, her 1967 recording wholly committed to it. Bergonzi, as always, is a model of style, and he is inspired by Barbirolli to sound more involved than usual. Panerai is a fatherly, characterful Consul, Anna di Stasio an unassuming Suzuki.

Butterfly's death is the supreme test of any soprano's performance. Scotto brings out all its pathos and tragedy, catching also the exalted expression Puccini asks for. Here, as throughout, Barbirolli, with the willing cooperation of his Roman players, proves himself a master at adumbrating all this telling and subtle score's emotion within a structural unity.

Recordings Discussed

*Callas, Danieli, Villa, Gedda/Chorus and Orchestra of La Scala, Milan/Karajan   HMV SLS 5015

Tebaldi, Cossotto, Nerozzi, Bergonzi/Chorus and Orchestra of the St Cecilia Academy, Rome/Serafin — Decca D4 D3

de los Angeles, Pirazzini, Bertona, Björling/Chorus and Orchestra of the Rome Opera House/Santini — HMV SLS 5128

Price, Elias, di Stasio, Tucker/RCA Italiana Opera Chorus and Orchestra/Leinsdorf — RCA SER 5504-6

*Scotto, di Stasio, Padoan, Bergonzi/Chorus and Orchestra of the Rome Opera House/Barbirolli — HMV SLS 927

Freni, Ludwig, Schary, Pavarotti/Chorus of the Vienna Opera/Vienna Philharmonic Orchestra/Karajan — Decca SET 584-6

Caballé, Mazzieri, Marti/Chorus of the Teatro del Liceo/Barcelona Symphony Orchestra/Gatto — Decca D68 DR3

© Alan Blyth

Purcell   *Dido and Aeneas*

ANDREW PARROTT

Almost ninety years ago George Bernard Shaw was asked to review an amateur Purcell-Handel concert at Bow in London's East End. 'Entirely unacquainted with these outlandish localities and their barbarous minstrelsy', he nevertheless set off (with revolver as a precaution for his hazardous journey), determined not to leave Purcell's great music to the mercy of his paper's other music critic. Although the Bowegians evidently did not do Purcell full justice, G.B.S. was delighted with the music. *Dido and Aeneas,* he declared, is '200 years old, and not a bit the worse for wear'.

For all the professionalism of the most recent of recordings, I wonder, nevertheless, whether ninety years later we are any closer to understanding how best to bring Purcell's wonderful little opera to life. The six currently available recordings, in chronological order and with the conductor's name first, are these:

Geraint Jones with Kirsten Flagstad as Dido (World Records)
Anthony Lewis with Janet Baker (Oiseau-Lyre)
Alfred Deller with Mary Thomas (Harmonia Mundi)
Raymond Leppard with Tatiana Troyanos (Erato)   ·
Steuart Bedford again with Janet Baker (Decca)
Sir John Barbirolli with Victoria de los Angeles (HMV).

Dido and Aeneas was first heard in 1689, not on the public stage but 'performed at Mr Josias Priest's boarding-school at Chelsea by young gentle-women'. Priest was a dancing master and, no doubt, one of his main aims in commissioning this work from Purcell was to show off his young ladies in a series of dances. A small string orchestra and the necessary male voices for the chorus and the part of Aeneas must have been imported especially for the occasion. Nahum Tate's libretto has often been ridiculed: such lines as 'Our plot has took, the Queen's forsook!' and 'Thus on the fatal banks of Nile weeps the deceitful crocodile' do not fall well on modern ears, but the plot is laid out with skill and economy. Purcell's music matches this concision perfectly; the whole thing lasts little more than an hour, which means that in performance all the details have to be carefully judged, exactly in place, and that all the music will, conveniently enough, just squeeze on to one record.

There are four scenes. Act 1 is set in Dido's palace at Carthage and we are plunged straight into the middle of the story, with Belinda trying to console the dejected Queen Dido, who has already fallen in love with Aeneas, recently arrived from ruined Troy on his way to Italy. Belinda, the Queen's serving-maid (or perhaps her sister), has four dance-songs as well as the recitatives, and hers is a straightforward role, to comfort and support Dido. 'Shake the cloud from off your brow, Fate your wishes does allow', she sings. Elisabeth Schwarzkopf is the surprising choice as Belinda on Geraint Jones's 1953 recording (reissued on World Record's 'Historical' series), which has the great Wagnerian soprano Kirsten Flagstad as Dido. Apparently Flagstad, well into her fifties, struck up a great friendship with the theatre director Bernard Miles after hearing his one-man send-up of *Tristan und Isolde* and their 'love-lotion'. The result was that 1951 saw the opening of the little Mermaid Theatre with Flagstad singing Dido twice nightly in return for a bottle of stout per performance. The subsequent recording wears its twenty-five years pretty well. It has the feel of a mature performance, rather than of one assembled in a recording studio, and, even when tempos are perhaps too slow, Geraint Jones keeps a firm grip on the proceedings. I have some reservations, though. Schwarzkopf apparently was not in the original production, and despite some good singing, she remains slightly detached from the rest of the performance. Also it is confusing to the listener that she sings the Spirit and also some of the Second Lady's music. More distracting though is Schwarzkopf's far from faultless English. All the other Belindas are fortunately English-speakers: perhaps the most winning of them is the bright-voiced Norma Burrowes in the most recent of the recordings, under Steuart Bedford. In the opera, words and music are supremely well balanced, as the poet Dryden recognized when he wrote that music 'has since arriv'd to a greater Perfection in *England* than ever formerly; especially passing through the Artful Hands of Mr Purcel, who has Compos'd it with so great a Genius, that he has nothing to fear but an ignorant, ill-judging Audience' – to which we might add 'and certain singers'. Fortunately, Flagstad's sung English is really very good, yet I imagine that reactions to her singing will be very mixed. The expressive scoops, for example, can become rather irritating, and there is an unfortunate dearth of conventional trills. But without doubt, this is very fine singing of its kind and Flagstad's beautifully poised performances paints a very noble Dido. I found it interesting that practically all the singing on this 1953 recording seems to belong to quite a different tradition from that of the more recent ones. In particular, Schwarzkopf, Flagstad, and their colleagues use discernibly less vibrato; they also cultivate freer, easier top notes (which need not lack dramatic tension), and in both respects, I think they have the edge over the more pressurized voices we take for granted today.

An American mezzo-soprano singer, Tatiana Troyanos, takes the role of Dido in Raymond Leppard's recording for Erato. She has an exciting and colourful voice and her Dido certainly has distinction; but her performance is not completely even and in particular it is marred by some unclear diction which made me question whether she was indeed a native English-speaker. Dido has only two set numbers in the opera and in the recitative English-speaking singers should have an obvious advantage – not that any of the recordings are as speech-like as I should have liked myself.

On Alfred Deller's recording, available now as part of the Bach Guild's Historical Anthology of Music, it is sheer presence that Mary Thomas lacks by comparison with Flagstad and Troyanos. Also, Deller's performance suffers from a bad edition of Purcell's music. His attention to the careful characterization of each little bit seems somehow to undermine the opera's continuity, and this is emphasized by an unfortunate patchiness of recording quality. The choice of a Dido can of course make or break a performance. The only British singer so far to offer both real authority and impeccable singing is Janet Baker who made such an impression with her 1962 recording for Anthony Lewis on Oiseau-Lyre and who has returned to the opera on Steuart Bedford's Decca version.

With Act 2 the scene shifts from Dido's palace to 'The Cave', where a Sorceress holds court, attended on by two solo witches and a chorus of witches. These are the clear descendants of the witches in *Macbeth*, beloved of the Restoration theatre, and Purcell accordingly gives them some splendidly theatrical music. On Geraint Jones's recording, Arda Mandikian makes a suitably hysterical Sorceress (even if the chorus is a little too nice) pouring out sheer hatred for Dido. Such scenes are so far removed from modern theatre that there is a strong temptation to ham them up. I think it is very difficult to get the balance exactly right. Deller shows two approaches side by side, with Helen Watts a straight, but quite effective Sorceress and an over-enthusiastic coven of witches, who inevitably end up as comic figures.

This brings me to the role of the chorus, which is elsewhere less obviously dramatic. Especially at the opera's conclusion the chorus acts more as commentator on the events and is by no means of peripheral importance. The standard of choral singing is highest, even if the quality is slightly anonymous, on the two most recent versions, Leppard's and Bedford's, although the sound of Leppard's choir is over-large for such an intimate work.

As for the orchestra, much of its work is in accompanying the dances that punctuate the opera. Again, the two most recent versions have streamlined, crisp, modern string playing, but none of the orchestras achieves the true lightness of touch that would have come naturally to baroque instruments. Some of the best playing can be heard in the Echo Dance of Furies that ends the cave scene, played by the Aldeburgh Festival Strings under Bedford; it is clean and efficient, if lacking a real will-o'-the-wisp quality.

From 'The Cave' the scene changes to 'The Grove' outside Carthage, where Dido and Aeneas are relaxing after a boarhunt. Dido's attendants entertain them in song and dance with the tale of Diana and Actaeon. 'Oft she visits this lone mountain', sings the Second Woman, her one song in the opera; it is most pleasingly performed by Eileen Poulter (for Lewis) and by Felicity Lott (for Bedford). Then as a storm conjured up by the witches sends the hunting party scurrying back to court, a false Spirit 'in form of Mercury himself' appears to Aeneas and commands him to leave at once for 'Italian ground'. Leppard introduces an organ at this point to support the voice, a simple enough touch, but one which is somehow at odds with Purcell's brilliant economy of means. Normally sung by a soprano or mezzo, the part of the Spirit is given by Deller to a tenor, which in an opera dominated by women's voices is quite effective. It somehow seems slightly perverse, though, to assign the role to a boy, as Bedford does – the opera was after all written for a girls' school – and moreover the boy sings in a completely dead-pan way, as though (to quote Shaw again) singing were 'merely a habit caught in church'.

Anyway, Aeneas is duly tricked and is left to ponder the consequences. 'All brawn and no brain' is how most people view the Trojan prince in Purcell's opera. Certainly, the role is not a grateful one, as there is very little to sing and consequently hardly any time in which to build a character. It is very much Dido's opera. Maurice Bevan sings the part intelligently for Deller, but despite a more noble voice, Thomas Hemsley on Jones's recording is not so successful because of flatness. Richard Stilwell paces the part quite well for Leppard, but to me his voice seems quite out of place in Purcell, while for Lewis, Raymond Herincx clearly opts for the cardboard-cut-out approach. The only tenor to tackle the part of Aeneas is Peter Pears, singing opposite Janet Baker in Bedford's recording, and a remarkable performance it is too. Pears manages to create a both a real character and a sympathetic one. The main reservation must be that his voice is now hardly that of a young warrior prince.

Aeneas's soliloquy appears to mark the end of the second act. No further music survives, yet the 1689 libretto has six more lines of text, suggesting a witches' chorus and a concluding dance. For this purpose two of the recordings successfully adapt music from other works by Purcell, though Jones does not end in the right key and the Britten-Imogen Holst edition used by Bedford has a chorus in the major key, which feels wrong between two short movements in the minor.

Act 3 opens on the quay-side, where Aeneas's sailors are preparing for departure: 'Come away fellow sailors, come away'. Shaw was particularly fond of this music and described it as 'that salt sea air that makes you wonder how anyone has ever had the face to compose another sailors' song after it'. The opera ends with Aeneas's departure and Dido's self-destruction. This of course provides the musical climax of Purcell's compact masterpiece, in the form of the celebrated lament, and this in turn produces outstanding singing from Kirsten Flagstad and, twice, from Janet Baker.

Before summing up, I must mention the reissue of Sir John Barbirolli's 1966 version with the Ambrosian Singers and the English Chamber

Orchestra (HMV Concert Classics). It has no pretensions to historical fidelity but compensates with an unfailing musicality, even when the tempos are excessively slow. Heather Harper's Belinda is pleasingly direct and consistently well sung, while Peter Glossop's Aeneas, though dramatically quite good, is to my ears vocally inappropriate. As Dido, Victoria de los Angeles is predictably more at ease in the set numbers than in the recitative, where her English diction does not do full justice to Purcell's music. It is not enough to have a well-known singer with a beautiful voice in the role of Dido. All the same, the performance is a memorable one and the real hero is Barbirolli.

The differences between Janet Baker's two performances as Dido, recorded sixteen years apart, are remarkably few. Her tone has become slightly less individual and, surprisingly, her diction a little less compelling. All the same, her singing of the lament in some respects is possibly even better than before. Ultimately it must be the singing of a Dido that dictates which performance of the opera, as a whole is most to be recommended and though I do not wish to underestimate the value of Kirsten Flagstad's historic recording, Janet Baker's combination of a truly distinguished voice and a native English tongue makes her her own strongest rival as the best Dido currently available on record. At this point it would be convenient to be able to say that Bedford's recording supersedes Lewis's older one, but both have their weak points of casting and of musical detail. It is disappointing that the new recording seems to offer merely a handful of theatrical tricks in place of any new interpretational insight. What I am saying is not that Bedford's version is inferior to Lewis's, simply that it ought to have been better. I suspect that a definitive *Dido and Aeneas* (whatever that may be) is still several years away. But in the meantime we have Janet Baker's two performances to enjoy.

Recordings Discussed

Flagstad, Hemsley, Schwarzkopf/Mermaid Singers and Orchestra/Jones	WR SH 117
*Baker, Herincx, Clark/English Chamber Orchestra/Lewis	Oiseau-Lyre SOL 60047
Thomas, Bevan, Sheppard/Oriana Concert Choir and Orchestra/Deller	Vanguard HM 46
Troyanos, Stilwell, Palmer/English Chamber Orchestra/Leppard	Erato STU 71091
*Baker, Pears, Burrowes/Aldeburgh Festival Strings/Bedford	Decca SET 615
de los Angeles, Glossop, Harper/Ambrosian Singers/English Chamber Orchestra/Barbirolli	HMV SXLP 30275

© Andrew Parrott

Verdi   *Macbeth*

ALAN BLYTH

Macbeth remains a great but problematic opera. The problems arise from the fact that on to the basic 1847 score Verdi welded the 1865 revisions, so – in some people's minds – effecting an unhappy compromise of styles. But if we look at just how carefully Verdi went over his score when he returned to it, we can surely discern how cleverly he integrated his new ideas with the old, very often improving on the first version without destroying its early inspiration. Indeed, throughout, the thrust of a young man's work is tempered by the experience of an older and wiser composer's hand. The result is a work of vivid, direct music-drama, wonderfully and individually coloured in its orchestration, Shakespearian in its dramatic psychology, and always responsive to the dour, dark deeds portrayed within. Even a moment that at first seems Verdi at his most inexperienced and 'rum-ti-tum', such as the little march that marks Duncan's fatal entry into the Macbeths' castle, revels itself on closer acquaintanceship to be eerie and empty in just the right way.

For all that, it is not an easy work to bring off in the theatre or on record. It does not play itself as, say, do its successors, *Rigoletto* or *Il trovatore*. It needs perceptive and wholly committed interpreters. One of the most maddening might-have-beens in the history of recording is the Callas-Gobbi set that was never made. Callas's records of individual scenes show us what we missed, and her inflections so etch themselves in the memory that they form a touchstone by which to judge her successors. Gobbi was intended for the second of the two Decca performances currently available, but fell ill before he could record it.

The Lady Macbeth in that performance, conducted by Lamberto Gardelli, is Elena Suliotis, wrongly hailed by some of us in the early '70s as Callas's successor. This is immediately apparent in Lady Macbeth's first aria of vaulting ambition to the throne. The manner recalls her great predecessor's, but only as a caricature apes the original. Suliotis's intentions are often admirable, but their execution is faulty, marred by woolly tone and insecure phrasing. Lady Macbeth is a problem in herself. Verdi, in his anxiety not to hear some fluting canary, asked for a dark, harsh, stifled sound, but that has often been made the excuse for any amount of melodramatic licence. The role's range is huge, and often Verdi exploits the colours of the lower registers, which has encouraged mezzos to tackle it. I still feel, though, that Verdi may have preferred a soprano, and one with the kind of forceful utterance, dramatic power, and command that Birgit Nilsson displays on the earlier of the Decca sets, conducted by Thomas Schippers. Throughout, she exhibits just that kind of vocal assurance, and more flexibility than one might expect of a Brünnhilde slumming it on the Scottish moors. But that is just the point; one too seldom feels that she has thought herself wholly into the role. Nobody could say that of the Italian mezzo Fiorenza Cossotto, who calls forth the minister of hell to incite mortals to bloodshed in the cabaletta of her first aria, and shows a relative ease for her kind of voice in the higher registers. It is she who takes the role in the quite recent HMV set conducted by Riccardo Muti. It might be said that her timbre is more *chiaro* than *oscuro*, more light than shade. She has a true grasp of the role, and sings it with firmness and lucidity, trills and all, and her rhythmic bite has true grandeur. Her rival on the fourth of the available recordings, conducted by Claudio Abbado on Deutsche Grammophon and emanating from La Scala performances, is another mezzo, Shirley Verrett. Here, certainly, is the occluded sound Verdi may have wanted, together with the intelligence that marks all Miss Verrrett's work. But unfortunately good intentions are not always enough. Her technical shortcomings, and the need to manage her voice, are too often obvious particularly in the early part of the recording. However, by the marvellous 'La luce langue', one of the pieces Verdi wrote for the revised, Paris, version, she is beginning to come into her own, giving it very properly as an interior monologue, in which she broods in the night on the need for more crimes after the murder of Duncan. She offers a definite presence and an involvement in the part, but she does not always sing the Italian language as to the manner born, as does Cossotto.

When we turn to the role of Macbeth, again it is the native-born Italians who have the advantage over their rivals. Nobody is going to dispute the intelligence of Fisher-Dieskau's Macbeth, opposite Suliotis on the Gardelli set, but that very intelligence leads him to a mannered, studied way of tackling the role that is foreign to Verdi. So is his dislikable habit of sharpening certain important notes. Indeed, with two such variable principals this version has to be put to one side, sorry as I am to lose with it its supporting artists, Pavarotti as Macduff among them, and Gardelli's honest, unobtrusive way with the score. The other non-Italian Macbeth is Sherrill Milnes, who sings the part for Muti. As with all this American baritone's work, much thought has gone into his portrayal and its vocal execution. He colours the role effectively and always brings to it commendable vitality and imagination, but his effects do tend to be externalized, the labour he has put into them too obvious. 'Mi si affaccia un pugnal?' (Is this a dagger I see before me?), he sings forcefully; but this monologue, so prophetic of Rigoletto's 'Pari siamo', is marked by Verdi to be sung almost throughout 'sotto voce' and in a 'voce cupo' – in a sombre voice. These injunctions are more faithfully observed by Piero Cappuccilli, the first of our truly Italian baritones, on the Abbado set. Cappuccilli's long-breathed, malleable singing of this part and the understanding with which he projects it are almost beyond praise. No doubt they are the product of studying it and interpreting it with the same conductor on stage, Abbado, who here gives him quite superb support, bringing out the marvels of the scoring. In the monologue Capuccilli truly presents what the theatre critic John Barber has described as a 'devouring enemy within'.

The other Italian baritone is Giuseppe Taddei on the Schippers set. Taddei scores over Cappuccilli at just one point where his fuller-toned voice tells more strongly, at the moment when Macbeth imagines he sees the ghost of the dead Banquo in the Banqueting Scene. Taddei's Macbeth has, in fact, much to commend it, not least its vocal opulence, but it comes in a set which must inevitably be discarded, because his performance and that of Nilsson's exciting but generalized account of his Lady cannot compensate for the cuts their conductor, the late Thomas Schippers, chose to make quite arbitrarily at various points throughout the score, thus vitiating the merits of his own intensely vivid account of the music. In dismissing his version, we leave behind a good Banquo in Giovanni Foiani, reduced incidentally to a *comprimario* part in the Abbado version. That important but subsidiary role is well enough taken in one of the two remaining sets. Ruggero Raimondi, for Muti, sounds in poor vocal state so that we do not regret his precipitate departure at the hands of the murderers, but Nicolai Ghiaurov, Abbado's Banquo on both stage and record, sings with authority, and he receives ample support from the conductor.

The tenor, Macduff, has little to do but sing one recitative and aria in as eloquent a way as possible. This lament finds a chink in the armour of the Abbado version. Placido Domingo, who, significantly, was the one principal not to take this part in the Scala production, sings the piece too vigorously, as a rather ordinary solo. José Carreras, on the other hand, on the Muti version, gives it just the melancholic expression Verdi demands.

In the last resort one's choice of a *Macbeth* interpretation cannot be decided by the casting of these peripheral roles, but by that of the central parts of the Macbeths and the merits of the respective conductors. Abbado and Muti are, these days, respective rivals in the field of Verdian interpretation. Their virtues are to some extent complementary. Muti, obviously under strong Toscanini influence, imparts a precision and vitality to the score that does not exclude the utmost care over those subtle, mysterious string figures that impregnate the score at almost every point. His speeds, more at one or other extreme than Abbado's, are usually precisely measured for the piece in hand and allow for some occasionally thought-provoking rubatos, and the total effect is histrionically strong and invigorating. Abbado is more severe, playing it long, and integrating one tempo with another. The start of the Sleepwalking Scene gives some idea of the thought behind Abbado's reading. The violas' and cellos' surging figure is marvellously related to the agitated staccato of the violins, while the cor anglais laments in just the manner asked for by Verdi. Against this perfectly imagined accompaniment and its steady pulse, Shirley Verrett seems to carry forward the vocal line in a single effort of disturbed dreaminess. In Muti's reading the faster speed just fails to capture the eeriness of the situation, the orchestral playing is less keenly pointed, the singing of Cossotto, although sharply inflected, is more obvious in its effects, and the recording, as throughout this HMV set, is more reverberant and thus less atmospheric than the tight, lean DG acoustic. The Sleepwalking Scene actually takes some twenty seconds less time than the Abbado version. Muti's set includes, as a supplement, and this is a point in its favour, three items from the 1847 score that Verdi replaced with more subtle music when he came to revise his work in 1865. However, the last of these, Macbeth's dying 'Mal per me' is also to be found within the final scene in the Abbado set, a procedure often followed these days in the opera house and one that I find satisfactory. In the other pieces in the appendix, Cossotto's heavy mezzo is not well suited to 'Trionfai', which originally stood in the place of 'La luce langue', as it lies too high for her, but Milnes copes magnificently with the exciting piece of baritonal show-off that closed Act 3 in 1847.

If you want these valuable additions, you will go for the Muti version. There you will also find the more fiercely characterized choral singing – witches and Scottish exiles strongly impersonated by the Ambrosian Opera Chorus. The Scala Chorus for Abbado provides a bigger but also more vibrant sound. Both versions have the ballet music, considered among the most telling Verdi wrote for any work, and finely played by both the New Philharmonia for Muti, the Scala Orchestra for Abbado.

I am left with admiration for both performances, and in certain moods I will want to hear the particular excitements provided by Muti and especially by his Lady Macbeth, Fiorenza Cossotto giving a most considered performance; she studied the part specially for this recording. But for the most convinced and convincing interpretation of this dark-hued opera, I turn to Abbado and his La Scala forces. Verrett's Lady Macbeth may have its uncomfortable moments but by and large she is a worthy partner in crime to Cappuccilli's sinister but very human Macbeth. In the murder duet, for example, which Verdi set so much store by that he rehearsed it 151 times, I doubt if even then it had any more atmosphere and intensity than is brought to it by Verrett, Cappuccilli, and Abbado, nor a closer attention to Verdi's markings, a consistent feature of this exciting, thoroughly prepared set.

Recordings Discussed
Taddei, Nilsson, Foiani, Prevedi/Accademia   Decca SET 282–4
di Santa Cecilia, Rome/Schippers

Fischer-Dieskau, Suliotis, Ghiaurov, Pavarotti/
   Wandsworth School Choir/Ambrosian Singers/
   London Philharmonic Orchestra/Gardelli

Decca SET B 510–2

*Cappuccilli, Ghiaurov, Verrett, Domingo/La
   Scala, Milan/Abbado

Deutsche Grammophon
2709 062

Milnes, Cossotto, Raimondi, Carreras/Ambrosian
   Opera Chorus/New Philharmonia Orches-
   tra/Muti

HMV SLS 992

© Alan Blyth

Wagner   *Tristan und Isolde*

JOHN STEANE

It is not surprising that nobody takes *Tristan und Isolde* lightly. If you go to see it, or if you buy a recording of it, you know in advance that a considerable expenditure is involved, both of time and money. The recording companies know this too: a new *Tristan* has to be an event. Similarly for the conductor; his *Tristan*, like his Ninth Symphony, his B minor Mass, or his *Otello*, is one of the supreme challenges. And for the singers too: since so few are able to sustain these massive roles, those who can must rise to the height of their art to give them the emotional range and depth they need. A special event then, and four special recordings.

The oldest is under Furtwängler, has Flagstad as its Isolde, and dates from 1953. Solti's was the first recording in stereo (1961), with Birgit Nilsson. Nilsson appears again, with Windgassen as her Tristan, in a recording from the Bayreuth Festival of 1966; this is conducted by Karl Böhm. The fourth and most recent is under Karajan: it came out in 1973 and the leading roles are sung by Helga Dernesch and Jon Vickers.

Now, it is almost an unwritten law of these reviews in 'Building a Library' that the final choice or recommendation should come right at the end so that there is a mild element of surprise. I think that for once I had better forego the innocent pleasures of this mystification, for something approaching twenty hours of music are under review and it is as well to declare one's position from the start. So I am going to say straight away which version I am recommending, and then explain why. Having lived with these records for some weeks, I find myself very reluctant to part with any of them, but the knowledge is perfectly clear and inescapable. I have a free evening ahead. I am going to listen to *Tristan und Isolde* in my own living-room, not in the opera house, and I am going to listen not for the interest of a particular part but for the enjoyment of the whole. The four box-sets are before me. I choose the later HMV set, conducted by Karajan.

The amazing opening to the opera, with its uncertainties of time and tonality gives something of the flavour of Karajan's treatment of the score. Very tender and very lyrical, it is also quiet in the sheer level of recording. Böhm in the same passage has more marked crescendos and a sforzando strongly placed at the climax point within the phrase. It is noticeably faster, and perhaps, in isolation, seems more intense. But Karajan has this great point throughout: that is, never to anticipate *the* climax. He prefers tenderness and yearning where the others heap the fires; yet in doing so, he works on our emotions more humanly and appealingly, and then when *the* climax comes, it is all the more moving, both by contrast and by having this fund of emotional human involvement gently, persuasively accumulated in what has gone before. In the continuation of the Prelude too, he brings out clearly and subtly the changing orchestral colours in the 'love-glance' motif where there is both passion and control in the slow, loving motion towards climax. Fine as the other performances are, they do not to my mind achieve this lovely kaleidoscopic change of colours or, for instance, the sense of gentle thrust with the entrance of the brass.

Furtwängler, with beautiful singing tone from the Philharmonia strings and a great feeling of involvement, was fine too, in his famous recording of 1953. But I think the point remains. The full realization of things in the score being just so, and not otherwise, is most specifically achieved by Karajan, with the effect that the emotional impact is even greater.

Now the singers, and first, Isolde. Two of the Isoldes are the same – Birgit Nilsson. They are also quite remarkably different. When she sang the role with Solti, Nilsson's voice was at its finest and she presented a very human Isolde. At the Bayreuth Festival, in Wieland Wagner's production of 1966 conducted by Böhm, her voice was less evenly produced and the characterization had quite a different emphasis. In Act 1 she is formidable, even sinister: the sorceress, the proud, angry princess, scornful and vindictive. This is the dominant feeling here, and it is vividly conveyed. In the passage where Isolde sends her maid Brangaene to Tristan, summoning him to her presence, her scorn is withering, especially as she shoots out the word 'Furcht' offering to teach the hero fear. In the earlier recording, with Solti, the effect of that and of similar passages is comparatively mild. In both recordings, of course, her Isolde is titanic in the big climaxes as in the great sequence of curses at the end of the Narration. There is nothing mild about it, in the Solti recording, when she pictures Tristan mockingly pointing her out to the King as a fine bit of adventure for him ('Mir lacht der Abenteuer') and then fairly lays about her. Solti's conducting here is immensely energetic, and that is one of its great features throughout the opera. Never does anything happen in the playing that is not alive, exact, and delivered with full concentration. It is a marvellous performance in many ways, and a triumphant piece of recording.

In such passages, moreover, Nilsson has incomparable brilliance of attack and knife-edge clarity and incisiveness; and in the role as a whole she is by no means without tenderness. Yet Isolde surely ought to be lovable, and I don't think it can be said that Nilsson's Isolde (either of them) is exactly that. An extra richness and depth of tone, an extra nobility of style: these are present in Kirsten Flagstad. She was in her late fifties when this recording was made, yet her voice is still gloriously warm and resonant, and she rises triumphantly above the orchestral floods. A fine example of her singing is the solo in Act 2, which reaches its climax as Isolde cries 'Let it be night that love may shine forth'. Then she bids Brangaene to keep watch and the signal is given that is to start the great love duet. In such passages Flagstad is supreme in her combination of power and warmth.

Yet even in the face of such magnificence as is provided by the combined forces of the greatest Wagnerian soprano and conductor of their age, I still recommend what Karajan and Dernesch have to offer. Dernesch presents a very different Isolde from Flagstad or Nilsson. I said that I did not find Nilsson's Isolde lovable, and in a different way this is true of Flagstad's as well. Flagstad's is admirable, generous and noble, but still difficult (as modern jargon has it) to 'relate to'. One *should* love her, as a character, yet she is beyond it. Dernesch, by contrast, *is* lovable. Her character in Act 1 is of a credible woman in a credibly anxious situation, being taken to a foreign country, and tormented by memories. This girl, as Dernesch presents her, *needs* Brangaene's comfort and help, and one feels that she has the nature to inspire such loyalty and affection in a servant. And when it comes to the love duet, then it is as to a true, very tender, as well as passionate, expression of love between two distinct and credible human beings. Her Tristan is Jon Vickers: the voices are rather more distant than in the other recordings and yet are heard in a natural, convincing stage perspective. Vickers and Dernesch also have plenty of power in their voices, but the full power is sparingly used and I think rightly so. Vickers is an extraordinary singer. There is so much to admire, yet I find myself repeatedly irritated by some of his vowel sounds, the 'ee's' particularly, and I sometimes wish there were more ring and resonance in the big voice. He is still the most human and responsive of the singers we have in this role. With Flagstad the Tristan is Ludwig Suthaus, who sings with more pleasant warmth of tone and sense of style than many German heroic tenors; even so, it is not really a distinguished performance. With Nilsson in the Solti recording is a rather thin, sharp-voiced tenor, Fritz Uhl; one is grateful for the definition of his sound and often for his vivid characterization, but there is little that is romantic in his tone or heroic in his stature. At Bayreuth in 1966, however, Nilsson was singing with Wolfgang Windgassen, and he gives a most touching performance. He was then over fifty, and his voice (which in his prime was singularly beautiful) had lost its freshness. But he rises to the gruelling demands of the third act like one inspired. Recording 'live' from the stage does at such times have a sense of occasion, and one is moved by the sheer stamina and spirit of the singer.

In some other respects, oddly, the 'live' stage recording is less atmospheric than the studio performances. The Steersman's song at the beginning of the opera, for instance, has a much better sense of distance in the studio, as have the hunting horns of Act 2. It is also rather curious that Christa Ludwig who is the Brangaene of both the Böhm and Karajan recordings, sings and acts notably better in the studio. She is not ideally firm, but in the Bayreuth performance, as recorded, is often tremulous.

Regina Resnik, the Brangaene of the Solti recording, also often lacks a really firm centre to the voice, which is what Blanche Thebom, with Furtwängler, has, though unfortunately she seems unable to match it with warmth or imagination. The other important roles are those of Kurwenal and King Mark, and again I find most satisfaction in Karajan's casting. The Kurwenal is Walter Berry, who brings a more pleasing, sympathetic tone and a better legato to the role than Waechter (with Böhm), Fischer-Dieskau (with Furtwängler), or Tom Krause (with Solti). Karajan's King Mark is Karl Ridderbusch, and he sings the often thankless role most beautifully. The long, long solo of Act 2 is the point where allegiance and endurance tend to be most often strained in the opera house. but with Ridderbusch singing as he does here there is not a note too many. Arnold van Mill is extremely good in Solti's recording, and Martti Talvela, rather rougher vocally, is still most impressive in Böhm's. On the other hand, Josef Greindl's unlovely singing is quite a serious flaw in the Furtwängler version.

To sum up, here are four distinguished performances, each quite individual. There is Böhm's from the Bayreuth stage, with the interesting later Isolde of Birgit Nilsson, and the Tristan, heroic in spirit if not always in voice, of Windgassen. This is a full-blooded performance, with plenty of forward movement, quicker in tempo than the others, and available in an attractive package with *Lohengrin* and *Die Meistersinger*, also from Bayreuth. Then Solti, with Nilsson at her best, and marvellous energy and concentration in the playing. The recording is fine, too, though the balance rather favours the orchestra. Furtwängler and Flagstad form a perhaps incomparably powerful combination; the rightness of feeling goes deep and that glorious voice is a feast in itself. The set is available at medium price, and the recorded sound survives well from 1953.

Even so, this is a work in which one is especially grateful for modern recording. In the Karajan we have that, plus a generally preferable cast in the supporting roles. The great joy of this performance, however, lies in its insight. It treats the score with that best kind of love; that is, the devotion which is always looking afresh, learning something new, gaining some new understanding. It presents a love story rather than an epic; it is dramatically convincing yet does not try to cram the opera house into your living-room; it works its spell upon the mind with quietness and restraint. At the moments of uninhibited giving, of heart and a full body of sound, it has plenty to give. It is a *Tristan* to live with.

Recordings Discussed

Suthaus, Flagstad, Thebom, Greindl, Fischer-   HMV RLS 684
    Dieskau/Chorus of the Royal Opera House,
    Covent   Garden/Philharmonia   Orchestra/
    Furtwängler

Uhl, Nilsson, Resnik, van Mill, Krause/Vienna
Singverein der Gesellschaft der Musik-
freunde/Vienna Philharmonic Orchestra/
Solti

Windgassen, Nilsson, Ludwig, Talvela, Waech-
ter/Bayreuth Festival/Böhm

*Vickers, Dernesch, Ludwig, Ridderbusch,
Berry/Berlin Philharmonic Orchestra/
Karajan

Decca D41D5

Deutsche Grammophon
2740 144
HMV SLS 963

© John Steane

Bach   *Four Orchestral Suites,* BWV 1066-9

LIONEL SALTER

No one knows for what occasions Bach wrote his four Suites (or rather Ouvertüren, which is what he called them), or even exactly when, though it is probable that the first three date from his time at the ducal court of Cöthen; the fourth was written either then or after he had left there for Leipzig in 1723. We do know, though, that he performed all of them at concerts in Leipzig, where he revised No. 4 a couple of times, drawing on its elaborate opening movement for the start of Cantata No. 110, *Unser Mund sei voll Lachens.* Each suite consists of a French-type overture followed by a handful of predominantly French dance movements, and this has led some scholars to maintain that these should be played as if for dancing. Others disagree among themselves about what these dancing speeds were. For example, one school of thought, following such eighteenth-century authorities as Affilard and Brossard, holds that the minuet was still a fast dance in Bach's time (as it certainly was originally); but it is an historical fact that all dances tended to get slower with the passage of the years – the most notable example being the sarabande, which started life as a wild licentious dance – and the alternative view of the minuet is that by 1720 it had got down to a very slow pace indeed.

As if such fundamental differences of tempo were not enough, in the seven current recordings of the complete Suites we are faced with that problem which nowadays inevitably arises with music of the eighteenth and earlier centuries – the question of performing style. Our contenders fall into three main categories: what you might call the literalists; the musicologically informed using modern resources; and the purists who insist on authentic early instruments, or copies of them, as a necessary element in securing fidelity to the composer's intentions. The literalists (that is to say musicians either unaware of, or indifferent to, the findings of research, who take the published parts as gospel and approach them with the same careful exactitude as if they had been written by, say, Mahler) are represented by two recordings from 1962: by Karl Münchinger with the Stuttgart Chamber Orchestra and by Karl Richter with the Munich Bach Orchestra. Münchinger, for example, finding that the opening of the Overture to No. 1 has no marks of phrasing or dynamics, plays it that way, with a kind of heavy brutalism that makes me think of the architecture of London's South Bank.

The second group, the modern stylists, has three runners, two of which come from the same stable. Thurston Dart's twenty-one year-old recording with the Philomusica unfortunately sounds its age now, but the performances are full of animation and imaginative ideas, even if some of these are slightly quirky. Lighter in texture than Münchinger or Richter (for the sets of instrumental parts preserved from Bach's time seem to point to single desks of strings), Dart went in for lively speeds generally, adopted the practice of double-dotting, and was adamant that the slow opening sections of the Overtures should be 'in 4' and not 'in 8'.

In 1971 and 1978 Neville Marriner, a disciple and colleague of Dart's, recorded the Suites with his Academy of St Martin-in-the-Fields along similar lines but adopting less extreme tempos. (In the first of these Dart played the harpsichord continuo – one of his last appearances in the recording studio.) Another recent issue of the Suites is also extremely intelligent and alert: this is the one by the Czech ensemble, Ars Rediviva, directed by Milan Munclinger, not to be confused with Münchinger. Technically, however, this recording is a bit boxy and lacking in depth.

Finally, there are two groups with complete authenticity as their aim, and both, in addition to employing historical detached-bowing techniques, play at a pitch about a semitone lower than today's norm. One of these is Nikolaus Harnoncourt's Concentus Musicus of Vienna; the other, which to be frank I find more warm-blooded, more musical in feeling, is the conductor-less Collegium Aureum, which to my ear, however, is placed in too resonant an acoustic for ideal clarity. Both Harnoncourt and the Collegium Aureum agree more or less as to how the Overture to the Suite No. 1 should be played, except that with Harnoncourt it is more cut up and galumphs along; moreover, in the quick section the ensemble, as Sir Henry Wood used to say, could have been more together. Both the authentic groups take the Forlane in Suite No. 1 boisterously – it was a Venetian dance that Casanova described as 'violent' – and it is ironic that Münchinger's Stuttgart Orchestra, which in general is so dogged and graceless, should wrongheadedly give the Forlane a slow gentle charm. Harnoncourt is at great pains to follow contemporary evidence: a comment by Georg Muffat that in a gavotte 'the second and fourth crotchets should be far more restrained than hurried' leads him to some most unusual accentuation.

The Second Suite features a concertante flute in its instrumentation: with one exception, the soloists in all the versions have been well chosen, and differences between them are not all that significant. The Second Suite is the most satisfactory of Münchinger's four, once you get past the laboured *grave* of his Overture: just occasionally you become aware that there is a (faint) harpsichord continuo, as in the Double of the Polonaise, where it plays a doubtful chord in bar 6. It is also only in this Double that the harpsichord can be heard in Richter's version, which also interprets the printed French overture rhythms exactly as written: in fact, Richter is so literal that at the first double-bar he even lets his cellos trill with an A natural instead of the A sharp obviously intended as the leading-note of B minor. He does lighten the tone agreeably sometimes, but on the whole I find him rather dull, and his Bourrée, for instance, is more like a brisk military march.

Of the two authentic teams, the Collegium Aureum is the better in the B minor Suite, despite being rather awkwardly balanced, with the bass heavier than the cello. Harnoncourt's group tends not to vary its tone much; nor is it always impeccably together. It is probably not his flautist's fault that his breathing is so obtrusively audible, but his solo in the Polonaise Double is disastrous because he keeps holding up the rhythm in order to gasp for breath; and this gives rise to the suspicion that Harnoncourt, most unconvincingly, takes the second Bourrée much slower than the first because his soloist cannot manage it. One rather odd feature in this set is that in the Sarabande – and in no other movements in any of the Suites – Harnoncourt suddenly decides to apply *notes inégales*; and his concentration on Bach's rich inner parts all but obscures the fact that in this marvellous movement the top and the bass lines move in canon at the twelfth throughout. Now you would think that any conductor would see to it that the two voices would match up not only in phrasing and weight but in matters of trills and appoggiaturas, even if these are not specifically indicated in the lower part (Bach clearly expected musicians to use their intelligence); but, unbelievably, this is the case only in Neville Marriner's performances. All through his performances of the Suites he never hesitates, in repeats, to ring the changes on Bach's instrumentation in order to vary the colour – a procedure which the literalists, and possibly the authenticists too, could frown on but which seems to me just what practical players in any age would do naturally; and like Dart also, in the repeats of the Sarabande Marriner lets the flute play without the violins in unison, accompanying it with single strings so that one can hear the canon played consistently.

The Ars Rediviva ensemble, whose vivacity is a strong point, also makes the canon plain, though without adjusting the bass line; and in the Rondeau it points the imitative figures well. It takes the Bourrée as fast as Dart does, and the Minuet even faster, which is saying quite something; the Marriner version with Dart at the keyboard is rather more restrained in both cases. Ars Rediviva, by adopting a lively pace for the Polonaise, slightly eases the task of its good flautist in his solo in the Double; but in this movement the palm must go to Marriner's soloist on both occasions, William Bennett. He not only produces a lovely sound (I realize that the authenticity school would object that it is characteristically modern, and that in the final Badinerie he exuberantly even throws in extra decoration), but in the Double he shows quite spectacular breath control, and in the Agro set it emerges in an all but seamless continuous line.

The Third Suite has always been the most popular, and its bright scoring, with three high trumpet parts and timpani added to the basic strings and oboes, suggests that it was intended for some festal occasion, though we don't know what. There are considerable problems in balancing the brass with a small chamber group of strings, which is clearly what is required: not even the most reactionary musician, surely, could want to return to the old symphony-orchestra style of playing this work. Münchinger lets his trumpets blare, particularly in the Overture, which is about as stolid as it could be, and Richter (whose double-basses sound like refugees from *Meistersinger* in some provincial opera-house) has rather tinny trumpets which, though not heavy, are piercing. In Dart's recording, which has a very constricted sound, the trumpets are not only raucous, particularly in the Gigue, but not well in tune. However, both the Academy of St Martin's and Ars Rediviva rejoice in discreet, well balanced brass.

Here is where the authenticists should be at an advantage, since their trumpets have a lighter quality; but they have intonation difficulties of their own, since on the valveless natural instrument the eleventh harmonic, which produces the leading-note in the much visited key of A, does not accord with the tempered scale. Another problem in this Suite (as in all the others except the Second) concerns the rhythmic interpretation of the Overture. In the French style, an upbeat figure of three semiquavers, we know, was crushed into half the written length. Most of our ensembles here do not even attempt this: Harnoncourt's Concentus Musicus does but is inconsistent, applying it to the violins but not to exactly matching passages in the bass. Only the Collegium Aureum shows how it should be done.

The most famous movement in this Third Suite is the Air for strings alone, which I do so wish could lose its popular title of 'Air on the G string', particularly since it is not often played today in the nineteenth-century arrangement that gave rise to that name. It calls for the nicest judgement in steering a middle course between the stonily inexpressive and the over-sentimental. Harnoncourt is the most boot-faced, with a bass line that could only be called dour; Richter, surprisingly, is highly romantic, and Marriner even more so, making endless rises and falls of tone or adopting an awed, hushed *adagissimo*. Ars Rediviva seems to me to get it about right, but its harpsichordist starts it with a splosh, apparently imitating one of Thuston Dart's rare misjudgements as a continuo player in the Marriner set; and then just when he *is* wanted, in the latter half of bars 3 and 4, perversely he fails to fill in the harmonic hiatus. The best group at striking a balance between expressiveness and restraint, I think, is the Collegium Aureum.

I like a lot of what Ars Rediviva does in the Third Suite, though the *presto* speed adopted for the Gigue, exhilarating as it is, is surely excessive, and there is an increase in pace from its nice crisp first Gavotte to the second which makes for an awkward gear-change on the way back. And while on the subject of the Gavotte, I must return to Marriner. As I mentioned earlier, he introduces a number of variants to the scoring. Thus in his 1971 Bourrée he allows the trumpets and timpani to join in only in the repeat of each half, which if not orthodox is very effective; and in the repeats of the second Gavotte he liberates the oboes from the violins, to which they have been yoked for the entire suite except for a dozen bars in the Overture, and lets them play on their own. More questionable perhaps is his addition of an appoggiatura to almost every minim in the first Gavotte in the interests of consistency, whereas Bach marks it on only one occasion.

For some reason the Fourth Suite (not published until 1881, nearly thirty years after the others) has never been so popular. Perhaps it is not quite so distinguished melodically, but personally I suspect that part of the trouble may lie in the work's proportions: a very long Overture (even longer than that in No. 2), followed by only three dances and a short joyful finale. This lopsidedness is accentuated when the fast section of the Overture and the following twenty bars of slow tempo are played twice over, which is what the Ars Rediviva and Harnoncourt do (they are the only ones to observe the long repeats in all four Suites). Mind you, it can sound interminable even without a repeat if taken as tediously as by Münchinger, who also makes the Gavotte leaden-footed, and chirps up in the first Minuet only to drop back to an unrelated speed in the second.

The start of Dart's recording, which now sounds very faded, is badly balanced, and his trumpets are sadly out of tune: his oboes too are nothing to shout about, though they are not as sour as in his First Suite. Harnoncourt's jerky-rhythm opening summoned up to my mind the irreverent image of a learner trying to drive a car with the brakes on, and again the Collegium Aureum is more convincing, though the out-of-tune trumpet G sharp makes me wince every time I hear it. For a buoyant 9/8 section Richter would be acceptable were it not for his over-exuberant trumpets; but for this section my choice is either of the Marriners or Ars Rediviva, though this last is not vividly recorded.

In the remaining movements the Collegium Aureum's performance is somewhat marred by imperfect intonation by the three oboes in the Bourrée and the Gavotte, and after an attractive jogtrot first Bourrée its slow-down for the second Bourrée, in the minor – just as in the First Suite too – strikes me as misguided. Harnoncourt springs a surprise by playing the Bourrée much faster than anyone else, but as if in compensation has a slow and elegant Minuet (which Ars Rediviva and Marriner both take very briskly). Marriner again uses his discretion freely with the instrumentation of this suite, omitting the trumpets and drums in several places, and in the Minuet letting the oboes and bassoon take the repeats on their own. You may think from these bald descriptions that he may be taking too many liberties with the music; but apart from the fact that what he does is entirely in the spirit of the time we must remember that Bach himself modified the instrumentation on more than one occasion. In the Réjouissance the Ars Rediviva is brilliantly ebullient but anachronistically fast, and for this joyous finale you could not do better than the earlier Marriner: the later one takes this movement (and the Gavotte of No. 4) more deliberately.

Apart from this, the other main differences between Marriner's two readings are that in the Philips version he gets down to solo strings (in Suites 1 and 4), takes the Forlane of No. 1 gently (with the oboe sometimes on its own), and in No. 2 follows Harnoncourt in introducing *inégalités* in the Sarabande.

I think it must now be clear that, apart from the versions which put themselves out of court through unperceptive performance or recording quality that is no longer satisfactory, a choice for a complete recording of the four Bach Suites depends very much on your personal tastes and your view of Bach. In every single issue there are points of interpretation or of tempo with which one may well be inclined to argue; but for all-round vitality, musicality, and freshness my vote goes to Neville Marriner's Academy of St Martin-in-the-Fields on Argo with his Philips version almost equally satisfying. At mid-price, Milan Munclinger's Ars Rediviva is recommendable, though the Supraphon recording quality comes nowhere near rivalling the others' excellence. And if you are a stickler for old instruments (even when they are not perfectly in tune) then the Collegium Aureum on Harmonia Munda is the set for you.

Recordings Discussed

Philomusica of London/Dart	Oiseau-Lyre OLS 104–5
Stuttgart Chamber Orchestra/Münchinger	Decca DPA 589–90
	(also available in 10-record set 14BB 213-7)
Munich Bach Orchestra/Richter	Deutsche Grammophon 2726 081
*Academy of St Martin-in-the-Fields/Marriner	Argo ZRG 687–8
Vienna Concentus Musicus/Harnoncourt	Telefunken AS 6.35046
*Collegium Aureum	HM IC 15199618–15189619
*Ars Rediviva/Munclinger	Supraphon 1 10 1361–2
*Academy of St Martin-in-the-Fields/Marriner	Philips 6769 012

© Lionel Salter

Bartók *Music for Strings, Percussion, and Celesta*

STEPHEN WALSH

The Music for Strings, Percussion, and Celesta is a fairly late work of Bartók's: not one of the works from his very last years in America, but one of a group of masterpieces he completed in Europe before going to the States early in the war. The other pieces in this group include the Sonata for Two Pianos and Percussion, the Second Violin Concerto, the Divertimento for Strings, and the Sixth Quartet. One of the features of these works is their investigation of instrumental sonorities arranged in families. The Divertimento, commissioned by Paul Sacher for the Basle Chamber Orchestra, investigates string sound, and the Sonata investigates percussion. In the Music for Strings, Percussion, and Celesta, another Sacher commission, the two studies come together, as it were. The score is a dazzling exhibition of group contrasts: on the one hand the strings, capable of smooth expressive lines and dense fabrics of harmony; on the other the percussion, hard and brittle for the most part, and fond of abrupt, emphatic gestures. Bartók sets the groups off by means of an antiphonal layout of the strings, to left and right of the percussion 'block' in the centre of the platform. But he also constructs a kind of continuum of sound. So we get a smooth progression from string tone made with the bow, through pizzicato and the plucked harp, to the pitched percussion sounds of the piano and celesta, the less distinct pitch of the timpani, and eventually to the peremptory unpitched sounds of the bass drum and cymbals. It is typical of Bartók that these effects are handled methodically, and indeed that the whole work is constructed with extraordinary precision. Parts of it certainly reflect an interest in the Classical Golden Section; for instance the proportions of the fugal first movement, as well as its key scheme, fit this theory well. Generally speaking in the '30s Bartók had got over the somewhat violent expressionism of a few years before, and had started writing in a more classical and more controlled style. But the music still basically hangs on a fragile balance between expression and form; and it is this tension which gives the Music for Strings, Percussion, and Celesta its great power.

Most Bartók lovers would number this work among his two or three finest, but it has never been exactly popular and at the moment there are only five performances of it on record, including – and this is perhaps the acid test – only one on a cheap label. But it is a particularly interesting work to study on record, not only because the engineers have a field-day with Bartók's antiphonal layout, but because Bartók worked out exact timings for each movement and even each section in the last two movements, and these are printed in the score, presumably for the guidance of conductors. Bartók's timings, in this and other works, are usually quicker than in the average performance. Possibly this comes from the composer's habit, when reading through the score, of hopping over unimportant notes. But it is more likely to be because Bartók worked his timings out arithmetically from his metronome marks, and that it is the metronome marks that conductors dispute. Take the first movement as an example. According to the composer this fugue moves within quite a narrow, but brisk tempo band – between 108 quavers to the minute and 126 quavers to the minute. Compared with this, Seiji Ozawa's quaver 84 in his recording with the Boston Symphony Orchestra is pretty slow, though it is more or less what we are used to. Why I wonder, does Ozawa not follow Bartók's instructions? Perhaps he is worried about the words 'Andante tranquillo' at the head of the movement, and one certainly needs to consider what Bartók may have meant by his marking. If this is tranquil music, it's the tranquillity of a deep and sinister mountain pool rather than of flocks in pastures green abiding. If we consider the same passage conducted by Sir Georg Solti with the London Symphony Orchestra, it seems that he has been at some pains to re-establish the authenticity of Bartók's own text. (One has to remember, of course, that Solti was born Hungarian.) To my mind, he fixes for certain that Bartók's tempo marking was correctly judged, and that a fairly brisk quaver motion does not in any way contradict the idea of perhaps menacing tranquillity suggested by the eerie chromatic style. Incidentally, this fugue theme acts as a kind of motto, and keeps cropping up in all sorts of different guises in the other three movements. The climax of the work is when it suddenly bursts through in the finale in a non-chromatic version – a very thrilling moment.

Coming back to the first movement itself, Solti is the only conductor who pays any attention to Bartók's tempo marking. But his two recorded performances are close together in this respect, so we still have a choice: between the London Symphony Orchestra on the full-price stereo version I have just referred to and the London Philharmonic Orchestra on a much earlier Decca recording, which comes in reprocessed stereo on the cheap Eclipse label. In both performances Solti generates enormous tension towards the climax of the movement. Yet I cannot really recommend buying this work in a cheap version, if only because it needs exact and systematic stereo recording. The London Symphony Orchestra string playing is also rather superior to that of the London Philharmonic Orchestra of nearly twenty-five years ago.

The other two conductors are Karajan with the Berlin Philharmonic and Neville Marriner directing the Academy of St Martin-in-the-Fields. It appears that Marriner actually plays in this performance, directing from the first desk. If so the precision of the performance is truly remarkable, because Bartók's rhythms are very irregular, even when the values are constant. In the first movement we find typically lucid, shapely playing, less urgent than Solti's, but somewhat more definite than Ozawa's and at a tempo about halfway between the two.

In the second movement, a strongly rhythmic Allegro in sonata form, the question of recording technique becomes really vital. Here and for the rest of the work the strings are laid out in the manner of a double orchestra, on each side of the percussion group; and moreover Bartók emphasizes this spacing by means of scrupulously planned contrasts in timbre. Again Solti gives an exemplary performance, beautifully supported by the Decca engineers. His tempo is close to Bartók's suggested figure, and above all not too fast, so that the rhythms are exact and articulation clear, apart from some trifling errors of ensemble. The sonorities here are exceptionally fascinating, and have the added virtue of articulating the form. Towards the end of the exposition the texture moves from bowed strings – in a swirl of chromatics – towards a more brittle sound for the start of the development. The change is heralded by a piano entry and by strings switching to pizzicato interspersed with strange glissando noises. Then the texture suddenly turns hard, with dry piano chords and that harsh rebounding pizzicato which was Bartók's own invention. (The theme at this point is an upside-down version of the first movement theme, though completely changed in character.) It is interesting to compare this Solti performance with the one by Karajan and the Berlin Philharmonic, where the tempo is marginally quicker than Solti's and the general effect more mercurial, with slightly more nuance between sections and phrases. However, the recording is less satisfactory, perhaps because of the greater resonance, combined, oddly enough, with less depth of sonority. For instance, the piano chords are too much dominated by the right hand and the harp is too prominent. But still the whole effect is exciting and full of energy.

The second movement responds well, of course, to the crisp, virtuoso treatment favoured by modern orchestras and conductors, especially perhaps in the USA. Ozawa's performance is noticeably harder and more muscular than Solti's and much more so than Karajan's; and clarity is given high priority by those responsible for the final balance. For instance, at a later stage of the development in this movement the timpani solo leads to a fugato based on a serpentine version of the main theme related also to the fugue theme from the first movement, the entries crawling up from the bottom of the orchestra in a series of fifths. These entries are *con sordino* and are by no means easy to articulate, but both they and the timpani remain perfectly distinct throughout this passage in the Boston recording. The same passage in the Solti version is much more nebulous and the timpani are hard to hear at all. This effect may of course be deliberate: the music certainly sounds slimier in this version, though one could wish for slightly more presence in the entries themselves.

If the second movement calls for a certain hardness of muscle, the third is essentially a study in delicacy and exact note-placement. This is another of Bartók's well-known night-music slow movements – perhaps in fact the most exquisitely refined and imaginative that even he wrote. Wisps of more or less familiar melody meander through the nocturnal scurry; but the actual texture is the main point of the movement. It is music which really comes from nowhere but Bartók's imagination, though one can find vague precedents in Debussy and perhaps Berg.

It is hard to choose between Solti and Ozawa in this movement: both do it beautifully. Perhaps Ozawa, with the marvellous Boston orchestra, secures the more polished playing, but the London Symphony Orchestra also acquit themselves superbly here and the playing has more character than in the Boston version. However, the greatest virtue of Solti's performance, here as elsewhere, is his remarkable gift for generating atmospheric tension, so that even music which, in traditional terms is basically static, still gives one the feeling that it is about to explode into violent activity; and again the quicker tempo helps. Compared with Solti, the temperature of Marriner's performance of this movement with the Academy of St Martin's is rather low. The playing of course is masterly. But here, and occasionally at other times in the performance, one feels the lack of what one might call a fully committed conductor: there is the material here for a great performance, but not yet quite the realization.

Approaching a clear decision over these different recordings, I feel it can be quickly boiled down to a choice between Solti and Ozawa. The other two full-price versions have nothing that these do not also have, and perhaps lack their very best points. On purely technical grounds I should probably choose Ozawa, a conductor for whom I have the greatest admiration. But this is not a clear-cut point; and in other ways there are good grounds for preferring Solti. Solti's speeds are generally closer than anyone else's to Bartók's, and, better than his rivals, he manages to combine clear, firm articulation with lightness of touch and variety of colour. Above all his performance has wonderful urgency and a continuous feeling of dramatic tension which is finally resolved at the great moment in the finale which I mentioned earlier. This is what, eventually, gives the performance its peculiar feeling of authenticity.

Recordings Discussed

London Philharmonic Orchestra/Solti	Decca ECS 553
*London Symphony Orchestra/Solti	Decca SXL 6111
Academy of St Martin-in-the-Fields/Marriner	Argo ZRG 657
Berlin Philharmonic Orchestra/Karajan	Deutsche Grammophon 2530 065
Boston Symphony Orchestra/Ozawa	Deutsche Grammophon 2530 887

© Stephen Walsh

Beethoven

Symphony No. 6
'The Pastoral'

ROBERT PHILIP

Some five years ago there were eighteen available versions of this symphony; now there are twenty-five, thirteen survivors plus another dozen (and that does not include ones that are available only in boxed sets). When one is considering so many recordings, the only thing to do is to draw up a shortlist of conductors to compare, in this case Karajan, Cluytens, Loughran, Schmidt-Isserstedt, Monteux, Böhm, Maazel, Jochum, Boult, Klemperer, Giulini, Kempe, and Colin Davis. This inevitably means that I am having to leave out a number of good performances. For example, there is a 1947 recording by the Rome Augusteo Orchestra under De Sabata, a performance of great warmth and impact, despite the elderly recording and some sour woodwind tuning. Reiner's version with the Chicago Symphony Orchestra has been greatly praised by some reviewers, but I find it rather lethargic, particularly in the slow movement. Solti's recording is impressively played by the same orchestra, but his characteristically aggressive accents in loud passages often seem out of place in this symphony, and his flexibility of tempo in the second and fifth movements sounds merely indecisive.

The greatest differences between the various performances are to be found in the first movement. Nor is this at all surprising, because Beethoven's indications are self-contradictory: there is a very fast metronome mark (minim = 66), but there is also the heading *Allegro ma non troppo* and the general title 'Awakening of happy feelings on arriving in the country'. Colin Davis conducting the London Symphony Orchestra on a medium-price Philips label suggests a healthy country walk. His is one of the fastest versions of the first movement, a bracing style of performance, which nevertheless avoids the danger of sounding breathless. I think Karajan is less successful in that way; but more of him later. There used to be in the catalogue a couple of recordings by Furtwängler which showed the exact opposite of Davis's approach – more of a sort of long, timeless dream of the countryside. Eugen Jochum, in two different recordings, is almost as slow as Furtwängler, but without the expressive intensity which made those old recordings convincing. To me, Jochum sounds dull and heavy footed in both of his two versions, with the London Symphony Orchestra on full-priced HMV, and the Amsterdam Concertgebouw Orchestra on medium priced Philips. Most other conductors take a middle course between these two extremes. Giulini, Cluytens, and Loughran give very spacious performances but avoid Jochum's heaviness. Kempe, Monteux, Maazel, Boult, Klemperer, Böhm, and Schmidt-Isserstedt give more lively performances though not as fast as Colin Davis. The differences between them are to do with phrasing, balance, and tone-quality, all very much a matter of opinion. My own view is that the most beautiful of these seven versions are the ones conducted by Monteux, Kempe, and Böhm. Monteux, with the Vienna Philharmonic Orchestra in Decca's cheap series 'The World of the Great Classics', combines a lyrical style of phrasing with a really firm sense of rhythm.

I have already mentioned a fast performance by Karajan, and I said that I thought he did not succeed as well as Colin Davis. He has two recordings at full price on Deutsche Grammophon with the Berlin Philharmonic, and there is really not much difference between them. He gives the sort of performance which I find tends to flow past without really making me aware of the full character of each page of the score. For instance, there is a marvellous crescendo in the development section of the first movement, where the violins play the same pattern over and over again, against a counterpoint of triplets in the cellos and violas. In Karajan's recordings this passes by without making much impression, because he combines a fast tempo with rather smooth phrasing: it is just a beautiful wash of sound. By contrast Rudolf Kempe, conducting the Munich Philharmonic Orchestra on HMV's 'Greensleeves' label adopts a slower tempo. But it is the quite different balance and his rhythmic clarity, with every detail audible, which make me prefer Kempe's version. There is also the point that Karajan begins each crescendo with the celebrated Berlin whisper, whereas Kempe observes that Beethoven's direction is *p*, the *pp* being saved for where it is really needed. To my mind Kempe gives one of the most beautifully balanced performances of the first movement. Quite similar in style, and equally satisfying, is the version conducted by Böhm on full-price Deutsche Grammophon, with the Vienna Philharmonic Orchestra; certainly this is one of the best of the moderately paced versions of the first movement. Monteux is equally good in quite a similar way. Maazel, Boult, and Klemperer are almost as satisfying, and so are Giulini and Cluytens in a more spacious manner, and Colin Davis at a brisker tempo.

In the slow movement there is again a variety of interpretations to consider. There is one very basic point, and that is that it is a long movement, which follows straight on after quite a leisurely first movement. This means that a conductor has to be careful to avoid two dangers: one is to let it fall asleep, and the other is to make it sound too similar in character to the first movement. Actually this does not have all that much to do with tempo. It is possible for versions of the opening of the movement to sound different in character, even when they are taken at much the same speed. This is true, for example, of the performances by Schmidt-Isserstedt,

Maazel, and Kempe. I find Schmidt-Isserstedt's cheap Decca version with the Vienna Philharmonic Orchestra a slightly lumpy performance: it does not give quite the peaceful impression conjured up by Beethoven's title, 'Scene at the Brook'. In particular the phrasing of the accompaniment is chopped up in a rather abrupt fashion. Lorin Maazel, with the Berlin Philharmonic Orchestra on a medium-price Deutsche Grammophon record, goes to the opposite extreme, phrasing the accompaniment very smoothly, and making the tune in the violins very quiet and withdrawn. Incidentally Beethoven's marking at this point is *P*, not *PP*. James Loughran on full-price 'Enigma' approaches the movement in a similar, very withdrawn manner. But Kempe, Monteux, Böhm, Boult, and Colin Davis, on the other hand, all have a firmer approach which helps the music to move forward the whole time. Kempe, with the Munich Philharmonic Orchestra, also provides an accompaniment that is beautifully judged, phrased in the way Beethoven indicates, but not too chopped up. There are several performances of this movement which are more leisurely in pace than those by Kempe, Schmidt-Isserstedt, and Maazel. I think the most successful of these, because they are the most lyrical in phrasing, are conducted by Giulini on full-price HMV, and Cluytens on cheap Classics for Pleasure.

The Scherzo, with the title 'Merry gathering of peasants', is not a crucial movement for differences in interpretation. Most conductors give good performances, with only minor differences in character between them. However, one interpretation stands out as unusual, and this is the version by Klemperer and the Philharmonic Orchestra on full-price HMV. The whole of the rest of the symphony is played with Klemperer's usual lucidity and strength, but his Scherzo is exceptionally slow and certainly strikes me as remarkably un-merry. By contrast, Sir Adrian Boult's Scherzo is suitably agile and vigorous, and the London Philharmonic Orchestra plays well on his full-price HMV recording.

In the famous 'Storm' Beethoven's metronome mark is surprisingly slow. So often he gives a marking which is faster than most people play the music, but here he gives 80 beats to the minute. This is roughly the speed adopted by Giulini, Böhm, and Davis, while other conductors take it quite a bit faster. The power of the movement does not depend on tempo so much as on rhythmic strength. James Loughran, for example, conducting the Hallé Orchestra gives a straightforward, sometimes rather cautious-sounding performance of the symphony, with a pleasantly natural recorded sound; yet he takes the 'Storm' rather fast, though not achieving as much impact as some other conductors. This also applies to Maazel's second and more recent recording with the Cleveland Orchestra on CBS, though his is a weightier performance than Loughran's. Giulini not only takes it slower, but he uses the extra time to give more weight to each thrust of the rhythm, and to convey a tenser atmosphere in the quiet passages. His version of the 'Storm' has great impact, and so do the versions conducted by Böhm,

Monteux, Cluytens, and Kempe. Boult, Davis, and Schmidt-Isserstedt are not quite as exciting. Of course, one reason why the 'Storm' has to be really shattering is because it leads straight in to the fifth movement, a Shepherds' Hymn, expressing feelings of happiness and thanks after the storm. The greater the power of the storm, the greater the sense of relief after it. One of the most impressive performances of the transition from the storm to the song of thanksgiving comes from Pierre Monteux and the Vienna Philharmonic Orchestra.

When it comes to making a final choice, I think the position is not at all clear. There are a large number of excellent performances and recordings of the 'Pastoral' Symphony. As an absolute minimum, I would have a short list of preferences comprising Böhm, Monteux, Giulini, Cluytens, and Kempe, and there are at least half a dozen more which are really very good. So I would like to emphasize that my final choice is a matter of personal preference. I suggest three performances: first at full price on Deutsche Grammophon, Karl Böhm conducting the Vienna Philharmonic Orchestra, a beautifully spacious and powerful performance, in an excellent recording. My other choices are on cheaper labels: Monteux with the Vienna Philharmonic Orchestra on Decca, a splendidly warm and gutsy performance; Kempe with the Munich Philharmonic Orchestra, a performance with a beautifully balanced and blended orchestral sound.

Recordings Discussed

Concertgebouw Orchestra/Kleiber	Decca ECS 549
Philharmonia Orchestra/Klemperer	HMV ASD 2565
Suisse Romande Orchestra/Ansermet	Decca ECS 781
*Vienna Philharmonic Orchestra/Monteux	Decca SPA 113
Berlin Philharmonic Orchestra/Maazel	Heliodor 2548 205
Chicago Symphony Orchestra/Reiner	RCA CCV 5053
London Symphony Orchestra/Davis	Philips 6580 050
Berlin Philharmonic Orchestra/Cluytens	CFP 40017
Berlin Philharmonic Orchestra/Karajan	Deutsche Grammophon 138 805
Czech Philharmonic Orchestra/Kletzki	Supraphon SUAST 50796
Vienna Philharmonic Orchestra/Schmidt-Isserstedt	Decca JB 2
Concertgebouw Orchestra/Jochum	Philips 6580 139
New Philharmonia Orchestra/Giulini	HMV ASD 2535
Royal Philharmonic Orchestra/Lewis	Decca PFS 4188
*Vienna Philharmonic Orchestra/Böhm	Deutsche Grammophon 2530 142
*Munich Philharmonic Orchestra/Kempe	HMV ESD 7004
Chicago Symphony Orchestra/Solti	Decca SXL 6763
Berlin Philharmonic Orchestra/Karajan	Deutsche Grammophon 2531 106

London Symphony Orchestra/Dorati	Fontana 6531 009
Royal Philharmonic Orchestra/Dorati	Deutsche Grammophon 2535 219
Hallé Orchestra/Loughran	Enigma 53545
London Philharmonic Orchestra/Boult	HMV ASD 3456
London Symphony Orchestra/Jochum	HMV ASD 3583

Bruckner   *Symphony No. 4*

RICHARD OSBORNE

The opening of Bruckner's Fourth Symphony is so magical that it is difficult to imagine it not making its effect. There is a danger, though, that the conductor will adopt too lingering a tempo: too much atmosphere and not enough architecture. If this happens, the symphony, far from being launched in its first paragraph, will merely be beached. Karajan, with the Berlin Philharmonic Orchestra, narrowly avoids this; but in seeking atmosphere he adopts a legato style of phrasing which leads the horns, on two occasions, to smooth over the important semiquaver in Bruckner's four-note theme. This is on Karajan's earlier (HMV) recording, made in 1972 and available only as part of a boxed set, coupled with the Seventh Symphony. Karajan's later (Deutsche Grammophon) performance, which is available separately, is much tauter and, by a hair's breadth, gives a greater sense of motion. Not so, alas, in the case of Daniel Barenboim, whose Chicago Symphony performance is disappointingly static, the music bottoming out from the first. This curious sense of rhythmic stasis recurs on occasions throughout Barenboim's performance. A quicker tempo is needed if the symphony is to be adequately launched, and a quicker tempo does not necessarily rob the music of atmosphere, as Eugen Jochum beautifully demonstrates, again with the Berlin Philharmonic Orchestra. In this performance, at medium price, Bruckner's shimmering string tremolandos are also used as a source of rhythmic energy; from the outset we have a clear sense of the music going somewhere. Perhaps before I go any further I should say that some of the more obviously outstanding performances of this symphony are available at medium price: performances conducted by, among others, Haitink, Jochum, Kertesz, and Klemperer. It is also interesting that these particular conductors, almost to a man, treat the symphony not as a romantic tone poem, but as a serene and virile symphonic drama. And Otto Klemperer conducting the Philharmonia Orchestra offers us both stunningly cogent orchestral playing and superbly balanced sound.

The next section of this first movement has a delightfully folksy flavour, and Bruckner asks for it to be played in a rather easy-going manner: *etwas gemächlich*. Mahler, who affected to despise this symphony, clearly learnt a good deal from it. But as with his own Fourth Symphony, catching that special, easy-going pulse can present difficulties to some conductors as it does, for instance, to Kurt Masur with the Leipzig Gewandhaus Orchestra. His is a rather pale East German recording, and the tempos strike me as being a trifle stiff and self-conscious. Admittedly, Masur is preferable to Heinrich Hollreiser, where the playing is scrawny and the rhythms unsure. But given a comparatively matter-of-fact approach to the symphony, I would certainly prefer Kertesz and the London Symphony Orchestra, if only because the orchestral playing is that much riper. Well as the orchestra plays for Kertesz – and this is certainly one of the better-played versions of the symphony on record – I find his interpretation rather unyielding, both in phrasing and in orchestral texturing. There is at times a kind of inadvertent stiffness. By contrast, Karl Böhm is deliberately severe, a performance instinct with grandeur. He is helped by some handsome playing from the Vienna Philharmonic, and by Decca's engineers, who, with little extra charge to the customer, have taken the liberty of spreading the performance over four LP sides. To my ears, Böhm has quite the right steadily treading pulse for the second subject; but he is much slower than either Masur or Kertesz, so any direct comparison would obviously be highly misleading and not do full justice to the force and architectural rigour of Böhm's way, for example, with the symphony's first big climax. His is a recording of great deliberation and strength; perhaps the most purely imposing Bruckner Four in the catalogues. For sheer unforced naturalness, though, there is nothing to beat a recent full-price version on Harmoni Mundi by the veteran German conductor Günter Wand, with the Cologne Radio Symphony Orchestra; there is a guileless beauty, a winning freshness and spontaneity about their performance which Karajan's supercharged Berliners, or the Los Angeles Philharmonic under Zubin Mehta, cannot always match, for all their evident expertise.

The second movement, though less imposing than many a slow movement by Bruckner, has an unforgettable quality all of its own. It is a kind of veiled funeral march, half dream, half reality; now imminent, now distant. Conductors, I find, either get it right or they don't. Furtwängler, who certainly does (in a live performance recorded with the Vienna Philharmonic in Munich in 1951), catches well the music's enigmatic loveliness. Unfortunately, though, there is a more or less permanent ostinato of coughs and shuffles from the Munich audience and, fascinating as Furtwängler's performance is, it obviously cannot be a first choice. Being a live performance, it is far from secure technically; the Vienna horns fluff the very opening of the symphony, for instance. Moreover, there is a cut in the finale. But nothing that Furtwängler did lacked interest and as a collector's piece it is certainly more interesting than Hans Knappertsbusch's performance with the same orchestra. Knappertsbusch cuts not only part of the Finale but part of the reprise of the Scherzo as well.

Karajan, in his latest performance on Deutsche Grammophon – by any standards an exciting performance in the first and third movements – seems to me too quick in this elegiac *andante* second movement. An over-reaction, perhaps, against the excessive romantic licence of his earlier, EMI recording so that the playing is wistful, perhaps, but rather quick, cool, and not a little dispassionate. Böhm is also disappointing; I find him heavy-handed in this movement; but Jochum is excellent, as is Günter Wand. And Kertesz is certainly sympathetic, though here and in the Scherzo some of the quieter horn entries and the whole of the flute line are poorly balanced. Klemperer, though, is as fascinating as anyone. As in the first movement, the tempo is fairly quick, but balanced on a knife-edge. Like Karajan, he communicates a sense of forward motion, but Klemperer brings out much more clearly the music's implacability, its stoic beauty.

After such sublime imtroversion, what about the exuberant extroversion of the marvellous Scherzo? Here, for the only time in the symphony, Klemperer is at his most monumental, favouring slower-than-usual tempos. Yet even here I find a kind of cumulative excitement about the performance. Karl Böhm takes a similarly imposing view of the Scherzo and the Viennese horns and trombones are even more idiomatic than Klemperer's excellent Philharmonia players. At the other extreme, Furtwängler, Wand, and Karajan give the music a fierce demonic energy, full of fiery concentration. They avoid the absurd speediness of Barenboim, and are better recorded than Jochum where there is some muzzy articulation and more than a suspicion of the engineers fading up the first climax. Bernard Haitink, though, strikes a characteristic balance between these several extremes. He catches all the headiness of the chase, something which Böhm and Klemperer tend to miss, while avoiding the brashness of the more virtuoso versions. I also like the mellow sound of the Concertgebouw horns and the obviously natural perspectives of the recording.

Before leaving the Scherzo, I must mention an intriguing point about its Trio – a delightfully guileless piece, which in the days of 78s used to be something of a musical lollipop. In most editions the melody is first carried by flutes and clarinets. Böhm's Vienna Philharmonic play it with characteristic understanding of the music's Austrian origins in what most people would agree is the authentic text. There is another version, however, which gives the melody to the oboe. This is much more rustic, and is adopted by Klemperer, in his Philharmonia recording. Like the late Deryck Cooke, I will not disguise a sneaking affection for the oboe version, which is found in the first of Robert Haas's two editions. It is the one followed by Masur.

Curiously, on Klemperer's earlier and very much less successful Vienna Symphony recording he uses clarinets and flutes. There is another significant difference, too, since this performance sticks to the original scoring of the symphony's final page – that is with the horns playing an accompanying figure rather than re-introducing the big horn theme with which the symphony begins. According to Leopold Nowak, Bruckner's own final preference was for a full re-statement of the opening melody. Klemperer, with the Philharmonia, Haitink, and Masur all follow this idea.

But there are advantages to be had from the more straightforward of the two endings, favoured by Robert Hass and followed by such conductors as Kertesz, Karajan, Furtwängler, and Böhm. Here, there is a sense of unvarnished triumph with no attempt to confer a spurious unity on the work by resorting to cyclic form. (Incidentally, if you want a score of the symphony, Haas or Nowak are both acceptable; but the Eulenberg edition, which has a cut in the finale, is to be avoided at all costs.) So much, then, for a handful of textual points. What I must now do is return to a central problem: that of reconciling the structural and imaginative elements – the architecture and the atmosphere – in the difficult outer movements. As so often with Bruckner, this is a problem which centres on the reconciling of the musical elements at points of transition. This leads me to my final choice, and with several fine mid-price versions available, I exclude the full-price Karajan version (excellent as it is, it does not quite equal the achievement of his recordings of the Fifth, Seventh, and Eighth Symphonies), and the Günter Wand. I exclude the Wand with some reluctance, for it is a subtle, persuasive account of the symphony, freshly, if perhaps rather brightly recorded.

That leaves me with Böhm and Jochum, representing the two extremes of architecture and intuition; then Haitink and Klemperer, in his Philharmonia version. Haitink gives a performance of measured good sense, quite well recorded. Böhm is much tougher and grander, but some will think Böhm sometimes takes an extreme view. Similarly, Jochum is much more imaginative, but his frequent changes of pace – inspiring as they are at times – do tend to undermine the structure; and though one can argue that certain passages can take it, the Finale often can't.

To have both Böhm and Jochum would be an eminently satisfactory solution, for between them they tell us things which no compromise version – not even the excellent Haitink – can really hope to say. Yet there is a version which seems to me, miraculously, to marry spontaneity with formal strength; which is neither excessively severe nor excessively free; and which, though it avoids virtuosity as an end in itself, catches in full measure the score's sonic grandeur. That version is Klemperer's: an outstanding performance and an outstanding example of Klemperer's sheer pragmatism as a conductor. And to hold this symphony together you have to be pragmatic. The performance is full of grandeur and guile, is superbly played, and is superbly recorded. Incidentally, the first and second violins are divided left and right, an absolutely crucial effect in this symphony where the string writing is often of a highly antiphonal nature. Above all, Klemperer holds the symphony together marvellously well, at the same time communicating to us a clear sense of the music's mingled serenity and splendour.

Recordings Discussed
Vienna Philharmonic Orchestra/Furtwängler   Decca ECM 685

Vienna Symphony Orchestra/Klemperer	Turnabout TV 370735
Vienna Philharmonic Orchestra/Knappertsbuch	Decca ECS 511
*Philharmonia Orchestra/Klemperer	HMV SXLP 30167
London Symphony Orchestra/Kertesz	Decca SDD 464
Berlin Philharmonic Orchestra/Jochum	Deutsche Grammophon 2535 111
Concertgebouw Orchestra/Haitink	Philips 6599 729
Los Angeles Philharmonic Orchestra/Mehta	Decca SXL 6489
Berlin Philharmonic Orchestra/Karajan	HMV SLS 811
Chicago Symphony Orchestra/Barenboim	Deutsche Grammophon 2530 336
Vienna Philharmonic Orchestra/Böhm	Decca 6BB 171-2
Berlin Philharmonic Orchestra/Karajan	Deutsche Grammophon 2530 674
Leipzig Gewandhaus Orchestra/Masur	RCA RL 25106
Cologne Radio Symphony Orchestra/Wand	HM 1C 065 99 738

© Richard Osborne

Elgar   *Variations on an Original Theme, 'Enigma'*

MICHAEL KENNEDY

The Variations on an Original Theme is the most frequently recorded of Elgar's major works, and the available versions represent the work of fifteen conductors, for Elgar himself, Boult, and Sargent recorded it more than once. Incidentally, Elgar's own second (1926) recording is essential as historic evidence, but I am excluding it from my final assessment because of its primitive sound. Several special problems face conductors of this work. On its own terms it is a marvellous set of highly ingenious variations, full of short and telling passages for solo instruments. So the orchestral playing must have a virtuoso element. But virtuosity alone is not enough. The work is, as everyone knows, a portrait gallery of Elgar's friends and of himself, so there is a strong vein of fantasy and picturesqueness. Each variation must be vividly characterized, but the conductor must not turn the work into a succession of vignettes: it has a symphonic outline; with slow introduction leading to a first-movement group of vigorous pieces followed by a central slow movement, a Scherzo and a summing-up Finale. One must not push this symphonic analogy too far, but it is a factor in assessing a conductor's general approach. The tone of the piece, and of most performances of it, is set by the statement of the Original Theme itself, headed in the score with the word 'Enigma'. Elgar admitted that this represented the 'loneliness of the creative artist' (we may assume in particular of the creative artist Edward Elgar) and he also referred to it as a 'dark saying'.

So there should be more than a hint of tension in the solemnity of this beautiful tune, which is in two contrasted strains, the first in G minor for strings only, with eloquent falling thirds and sevenths, the second in the major, with descending fourths and fifths. At the repetition there is a counter-theme in violas and cellos, the first of dozens of poetic moments which give the work its emotional power. Elgar himself, in his second recording (the first, incidentally, made in 1920–1, was an acoustical recording, and the sound is consequently rather poor propounds the 'Enigma' very romantically, complete with the portamento string playing of that era. His metronome speed is well below the 63 of the score, but then Elgar's metronome marks are notoriously approximate and are certainly not canonical. Sir Georg Solti, whose undoubted enthusiasm for Elgar's music is so welcome in a musician who has adopted British nationality, shows his close study of Elgar's own interpretation, even to some portamento. Sir John Barbirolli, with the Philharmonia Orchestra, minutely observes every accent and dynamic, but less heavily than Solti; and he comes closer than Solti, I think, to the 'dark saying'. Nearer to Elgar's tempo, too.

The first variation represents Elgar's wife, and is an expansion of the theme with romantic and delicate additions. The theme is heard at first in the woodwind and the scoring shows that it is meant to be heard. Eugen Jochum and the London Symphony Orchestra, in a performance that is painstaking rather than inspired, rather miss this point here by being too matter-of-fact, whereas both Barbirolli and Sir Adrian Boult give the wood-wind prominence and suggest the feminine grace and stateliness of the variation. Boult, in his later version of 1971 with the London Symphony Orchestra (HMV) almost elevates Mrs Elgar, as she was in 1898, to be Duchess of Malvern. His is a splendid recording though it is not my first choice because, compared with his recent interpretations of the symphonies, it is slightly undercharacterized, and the Finale, where the extrovert and defiant side of Elgar is shown, lacks an essential fieriness. Even so, you can't go far wrong with it. The third outstanding English Elgar conductor of what one might call the second generation, Sir Malcolm Sargent, in the second and better of his recordings (HMV) rather spoils the effect of this first variation by giving too much prominence to the tremolo in the second violins and violas so that for a startling second one thinks one is hearing guitars. Sargent is too fast, too, I think, in the *allegretto* third variation, though he can claim to be nearer the metronome mark than Elgar himself. The charm of the oboe theme, with its bassoon counterpoint, is intended to depict an amiably eccentric friend of Elgar. Sargent, unlike the composer, makes him merely fussy.

People sometimes write about 'traditional' performances of the 'Enigma' Variations, but I am never quite sure what they mean by traditional. If they mean Elgar's performance, then his recording merely proves that sub-sequent conductors have nearly all moved slightly away from his approach. Most of them take two or three minutes longer over the whole work, so that there is no such thing as a traditional tempo. Take, for example, the fourth variation, 'W.M.B.', where the brass first get their chance: this is a very forthright picture of W. M. Baker, a Victorian country squire, *allegro di moto* and a rhythmic alteration of the theme. Here I find Zubin Mehta, conducting the Los Angeles Philharmonic Orchestra almost brutally off-hand in his treatment. It is, in fact, a performance of high voltage throughout. We can tell from his own recording how Elgar saw 'W.M.B.', with just a faint hint of mockery: his performance is much better humoured, and if you happen to have this version you will notice the very skilful rubato of the last two bars.

Elgar himself is as exciting as anyone in the first *presto* variation, Troyte (A. Troyte Griffith, a Malvern architect), with the timpani, cellos, and basses tumbling over themselves in boisterous energy. Among modern recordings Norman Del Mar's with the Royal Philharmonic has the same kind of rumbustiousness and also brings out the full flavour of the *brillante* runs on the violins, and of recordings by the post-war generation of English conductors I like Del Mar's the best. It is rich, warm, and brilliantly played. I have two reservations: first, that it was recorded in the over-resonant acoustic of Guildford Cathedral; second, and more important, the interpretation stresses the extrovert side of the music at the expense of some inward poetry. The recordings by the two Davises, Colin and Andrew, are faithful accounts of the score but I do not find that they linger in the mind for any specific virtues or insights, though I should mention that Andrew Davis's record with the New Philharmonia has one of the best balances when the organ joins the orchestra.

The best-known variation is, of course, 'Nimrod', Elgar's tribute to his encourager at Novello's, August Jaeger, and at the same time a memory of a conversation they once had about Beethoven slow movements, hence the reference to the Pathétique Sonata. But over the years this original association has become overlaid with memories of the Cenotaph service in Whitehall and various funeral elegies. The conductor must convey this nobility (Elgar did not mark it *nobilmente*, as he didn't use that term until 1901, but it *is nobilmente* nevertheless) and he must also stress the element of intimate and understanding friendship. This *adagio* begins *ppp* for strings alone and, as in the statement of the theme, a wonderful counterpoint grows in the lower strings. Jochum goes so slowly that he becomes prosaic, but Daniel Barenboim does this passage sensitively with the London Philharmonic, and his performance is highly recommended. Its principal fault, if that's the word, is that it makes each variation a polished gem at the expense of overall cohesiveness. The climax of 'Nimrod' comes with the repetition of the theme on the full orchestra, with strings and woodwind and most of the brass marked *legatissimo*. This flowing style, leading to the broad peroration in which the music suddenly subsides from *fortissimo* to *pianissimo* is eloquently done by Barbirolli and the Philharmonia. The firmly controlled playing at the end pays dividends in emotional commitment.

Similar intensity to Barbirolli's is to be found in Elgar's performance and in those of Leopold Stokowski with the Czech Philharmonic, recorded at a public concert, and of Pierre Monteux with the London Symphony Orchestra. Monteux is especially good in the five variations with women as the subject. Perhaps only a Frenchman could make Dorabella's fluttering oboes and clarinets quite so delicious and so clearly articulated and he has a beautiful viola solo, too. But Barbirolli, with a faster tempo, comes nearer to Elgar's own winsome picture of Dora Penny, with her suggestion of a stammer. And the Philharmonia's violist is even better than the London Symphony Orchestra's.

The 'B.G.N.' variation needs glorious string tone, provided by Bernard Haitink and the London Philharmonic Orchestra, in particular. And another crucial passage occurs in the Romanza, the thirteenth variation. Ostensibly this is connected with Lady Mary Lygon who sailed for Australia in 1899. The timpani imitate the throbbing of the liner's engines and the clarinet quotes a fragment of Mendelssohn's *Calm Sea and Prosperous Voyage*. But the music suddenly darkens, the harmonic mists close in, and the tragic nature of this episode suggests that Elgar was thinking of some other parting which had rent him in twain. It lasts only eight bars, but the score at this point is peppered with instructions. This black cloud passes as suddenly as it came – Elgar's music has several passages like this, the transition from the fugue to the allegro in the Introduction and Allegro for Strings, for example, and, even more memorable, the return to the main theme of the third movement of the Second Symphony after that terrifyingly violent outburst. Hearing Elgar himself in the 'Enigma' Romanza, though recorded over fifty years ago, one can still feel its powerful significance for him personally. Stokowski's performance, which is full of eccentricities, is nevertheless required listening for Elgarians because of the sudden shafts of illumination he directs to passages we take for granted. Unfortunately he ruins the magnificent effect of the tragic episode in the Romanza by ignoring Elgar's 'come prima' and sentimentalizing the subsequent clarinet solo. The whole episode is even more dramatic in Barbirolli's recording, on which the Philharmonia's clarinettist observes the *ppp* marking when the Mendelssohn quotation returns and the *pppp* of the very last note.

In general the Variations have fared very well in the recording studio. None of the performances under review is unacceptable, and several are outstandingly good. Elgar's own, as I have said, is a special case. The Monteux is superb, so, in their differing ways, are Boult's, Del Mar's, and Haitink's. Sir Charles Groves and the Royal Liverpool Philharmonic also give a fine account. If you want a vivid performance above all else then Monteux and Del Mar take a lot of beating. But my final recommendation is for Barbirolli's with the Philharmonia Orchestra. It is gloriously played, and Barbirolli is meticulous in his attention to detail, especially in the innumerable subtleties of string playing. Some of his tempos may be questioned in relation to Elgar's own, but are we to take Elgar's profusion of markings as restrictive or as spurs to individual imagination? I find Barbirolli's the most satisfying and moving performance because he captures the perennial freshness of the music, and at the same time a period sense: the Edwardian overtones are there but are not exaggerated. He conveys the beauty and originality of the scoring, but at no time is his interpretation a collection of miniatures. It is a portrait gallery with living figures, big, noble, and cohesive – a heartfelt affirmation of faith in the work which led Bernard Shaw to say 'English music has done it at last'.

Recordings Discussed

Symphony Orchestra/Elgar   Pearl GEM 114

Royal Albert Hall Orchestra/Elgar	WRSH 162
London Symphony Orchestra/Sargent	Decca ECS 588
London Symphony Orchestra/Monteux	Decca SPA 121
*Philharmonia Orchestra/Barbirolli	HMV ASD 548
Philharmonia Orchestra/Sargent	HMV SXLP 20007
London Symphony Orchestra/C. Davis	Philips 6580 265
London Symphony Orchestra/Boult	HMV ASD 2750
London Philharmonic Orchestra/Boult	CFP 40022
Los Angeles Philharmonic Orchestra/Mehta	Decca SXL 6592
Czech Philharmonic Orchestra/Stokowski	Decca PFS 4338
London Philharmonic Orchestra/Haitink	Philips 6500 481
London Symphony Orchestra/Jochum	Deutsche Grammophon 2530 586
New Philharmonia Orchestra/A. Davis	Lyrita SRCS 77
Royal Philharmonic Orchestra/Del Mar	Deutsche Grammophon 2535 217
Chicago Symphony Orchestra/Solti	Decca SXL 6795
London Philharmonic Orchestra/Barenboim	CBS 76529
Royal Liverpool Philharmonic Orchestra/Groves	HMV ASD 3417

© Michael Kennedy

Rimsky-Korsakov   *Sheherazade*

RICHARD OSBORNE

'Listen to *Sheherazade* symphonically and your imagination will be set free to roam where it will.' That was Rimsky-Korsakov's advice to us in his autobiography, in a passage which seems to predict Debussy's methods in *La Mer*. In effect, *Sheherazade* is a kaleidoscopic symphony of fairy-tale wonders. The first movement is a splendidly observed seascape, yet it is also an important piece of musical exposition; and the conductor needs to do justice to both these elements. If the underlying pulse is too slow, the music can seem portentous and dull, as indeed it does in an André Previn recording of the 1960s, and would do under Paul Kletzki were the playing of the Philharmonia Orchestra not so gloriously coloured. On the other hand, a good tempo accompanied by no real sense of fantasy is an equally serious drawback; examples are a Czech Philharmonic recording conducted by Oscar Danon and one for Decca by the Cleveland Orchestra conducted by Lorin Maazel. Imposing though Maazel's recording is, it sounds curiously functional when heard alongside, say, Sir Thomas Beecham's. Beecham's performance is symphonically stronger. By holding the heavy brass in reserve, he conjures a greater sense of foreboding as the climax comes into view. And the climax itself is expansive and glowing, much less laconic than in Maazel's reading. Above all, Beecham's view of the music is that much more picturesque. By placing greater stress on the upper strings and woodwinds, he seems to catch the very fleck of foam on the ship's bow. Beecham's performance is on HMV's mid-price Concert Classics label: the sound has been re-mastered, with the result that what was once a rather pale recording is now superb in its blend of richness and clarity. No one conducts this first movement better than Beecham; though Haitink is also very fine. He, too, builds the climaxes with great skill. It is a subtle, civilized performance, with playing and recording to match.

Not until the second movement do the important solo orchestral contributions really begin. This is a movement full of passion and caprice, the most atmospheric and various of Sheherazade's four tales. Taking, as it were, a hawk's eye view of the movement it strikes me as being quite the trickiest of the four to bring off. Herbert von Karajan, for instance, draws tone of byzantine splendour from the Berlin Philharmonic, yet in the latter stages of the movement there is a certain want of spontaneity as the pulse oscillates backwards and forwards. If only that could be put right in a re-make of this 1965 Deutsche Grammophon performance, then we would have something very special indeed. Similarly, though Paul Kletzki, again on HMV Concert Classics, draws much vivid and stylish playing from the Philharmonia, his performance is spoiled by moments of precipitate haste. The bassoon cadenza, for instance, is perhaps less stylish than on several rival versions and disappointing when what precedes it is so thoroughly alluring. In Haitink's full-price Philips version, we find a beautifully integrated recording, and a bassoon solo which is superbly played. Unfortunately, Haitink lacks something of the sheer swagger and style of a Beecham or a Kletzki in the march itself. Even so Haitink's performance is poised and unhectoring, and it is distinguished throughout by the fine quality of the London Philharmonic Orchestra's solo wind playing.

Some collectors may well be looking for a performance which is just that little bit smarter and brighter, in which case they would be well advised to try Seiji Ozawa in his latest recording of *Sheherazade,* with the Boston Symphony Orchestra. The Gallic elegance of his performance reminds me of the interpretation of another conductor closely associated with the Boston Symphony: Pierre Monteux, whose own performance of *Sheherazade* with the London Symphony Orchestra is still very much with us. Before considering Monteux's performance, though, what conclusions can be drawn about the second movement? Well, to find playing as stylish as Kletzki's is at its best, yet with solo wind contributions as sensitive as in Haitink's performance, we must return to Sir Thomas Beecham. Apart from a highly idiosyncratic bassoon solo right at the start of the movement, his is a near faultless performance with its special blend of delicacy and panache.

The third movement is an exquisite, lyrical *andantino*. Here Monteux is the only conductor to observe Rimsky-Korsakov's comparatively quick metronome mark. With a handful of notable exceptions – Beecham, Ozawa, Karajan, Ansermet in his earlier and livelier Paris recording – conductors do tend to make rather a meal of this essentially winsome melody, none more so than Leopold Stokowski. His 1964 Decca recording is actually re-orchestrated in places, a harp, for instance, over-riding the delicate clarinet arpeggio near the start of the movement. Never was lily so gilded. Stokowski's more recent, RCA recording is texturally purer but there is still a maddening array of expressive nuances to put up with. Fascinating as the playing undoubtedly is, it seems to me some way both from the letter and the spirit of Rimsky's wistful *andantino*. Stokowski may be a law unto himself in *Sheherazade,* but he is never uninteresting, which is more than can be said of Zubin Mehta in his performance of this movement with the Los Angeles Philharmonic. Nor does Stokowski ever descend to that baffling mixture of blandness and vulgarity which so characterizes Eugene Ormandy's performances on CBS Classics. But at least Ormandy has the courage of his own misplaced convictions. Towards the end of the movement he makes a substantial cut – a generous public admission that at so slow a tempo the music does indeed become stultifyingly dull. For not only does a slow tempo rob the music of its wistfulness and charm, it also makes it seem unduly repetitive. As Ansermet demonstrates in his 1955 Paris Conservatoire performance, on Decca Eclipse, the repeated arpeggios on wind and strings should be nothing more than delicate veils of sound, like the quiet murmurings of an Aeolian harp caressed by a summer's breeze.

Then there is the further question of how to link this opening paragraph to the movement's deft and gracious central section. Rimsky-Korsakov asks for this to go just a tiny bit quicker – *pochissimo più mosso*. Ansermet is good here, but Monteux is even better. He gives us some magical playing, and the kind of effortless transition which a slower tempo inevitably precludes. Among conductors who treat that principal melody *adagio* rather than *andantino* only Fritz Reiner really convinces me. Reiner's performance, made with the Chicago Symphony in 1960 and now available very cheaply indeed on Camden Classics, is in some ways a very studied one. Yet such is the eloquence and discipline of the music-making that, rather like the wicked Sultan bemused by Sheherazade, I find myself listening spellbound. Judged objectively, the shift of tempo and perspective at the reprise is, I admit, quite monstrous; yet the performance is hypnotically compelling. You may not care for so Germanic an approach, but it is a fine performance, worth bearing in mind if you don't want to spend a lot of money on *Sheherazade*. It costs a little less than Rudolf Kempe's Royal Philharmonic recording on 'Classics for Pleasure', another fine performance in the German tradition. The Kempe is marginally better recorded but ultimately it lacks the magical quality which makes the Reiner so strangely compelling an experience.

At the moment the only Russian conductor currently represented in the catalogues is Rostropovich. He gives an erratic, grandiloquent account of the score which the Paris Orchestra plays (HMV), at best sumptuously, at worst sketchily. Sometimes the playing is inarticulate, with stuttering brass, and as the movement unfolds, some awkward, unstylish string playing, where in spite of a poor precedent set in an earlier Chicago recording, Ozawa, with the Boston Symphony Orchestra, is stylish and direct. Perhaps a shade too direct. The opening flute theme with its rocking dotted quavers and contrasting triplets is nicely nursed, but later on the changes of rhythmic direction which give this 'Festival at Baghdad' much of its diversity and character tend to be rather brushed aside, the high-speed Boston train racing heedlessly across the points. Monteux, whose performance costs half as much as Ozawa's, is more careful of the composer's changes of rhythmic direction; but he is also, I must admit, a good deal less exciting. Indeed, it is by no means easy to get the rhythms of this movement right. 'Just a *little* more heavily' writes Rimsky-Korsakov as the music crosses over into triple time; but it is arguable that Bernard Haitink slows down too much.

Beecham again shows how the music really should go, with racing trumpets, beautifully accommodated cross rhythms and wonderfully guileful pointing of the big tunes. He even contrives to make the race to the big climax skip and dance. Throughout this Finale, Beecham seems to be echoing Caliban – 'the isle is full of noises, sounds, and sweet airs that delight and hurt not'. And as if that were not enough, there is one final, transforming touch in Beecham's interpretation. Most performances are so awash with sound at this point – it is, after all, shipwreck music – that most conductors quite fail to bring out what I can only call the Sibelian splendour of Rimsky-Korsakov's brass writing. Ansermet in his Paris performance, Karajan, and Previn all hint at this; but it is Beecham alone who, as the music switches gloriously back into E major, catches the writing for brass choir in all its glinting Nordic splendour.

Those on the tightest budget of all should, I think, go for Fitz Reiner. For those who insist on paying full price for their records: Haitink on Philips or Ozawa on DG. But for those who simply want a great interpretation, superbly played and resplendently recorded, then Beecham seems to me a clear first choice, not only for the bravura and splendour of the reading, but for its style, its delicacy, its imagination. Beecham knew and loved the all too neglected fantasy world of Rimsky-Korsakov's operas. Above all, he admired Rimsky-Korsakov as a craftsman, setting him alongside Tchaikovsky in his own private pantheon of late nineteenth-century Russian masters. All this is to be heard in Beecham's performance of *Sheherazade,* magical and vital from first note to last.

Recordings Discussed

*Royal Philharmonic Orchestra/Beecham	HMV SXLP 30253
London Symphony Orchestra/Monteux	Decca SPA 89
Paris Conservatoire Orchestra/Ansermet	Decca ECS 735
Suisse Romande Orchestra/Ansermet	Decca SDD 496
Philharmonia Orchestra/Kletzki	HMV SXLP 20026
London Symphony Orchestra/Stokowski	Decca PFS 4062
*Chicago Symphony Orchestra/Reiner	RCA CCV 5010
Royal Philharmonic Orchestra/Kempe	CFP 174
Czech Philharmonic Orchestra/Danon	Supraphon 1 10 1009
*London Philharmonic Orchestra/Haitink	Philips 6500 410
Los Angeles Philharmonic Orchestra/Mehta	Decca SXL 6731
Orchestre de Paris/Rostropovich	HMV ASD 3047
Royal Philharmonic Orchestra/Stokowski	RCA ARL 11182
*Boston Symphony Orchestra/Ozawa	Deutsche Grammophon 2530 972
Cleveland Orchestra/Maazel	Decca SXL 6874
London Symphony Orchestra/Previn	RCA GL 42703
Philadelphia Orchestra/Ormandy	CBS 30095

© Richard Osborne

Schubert   *Symphony No. 8 in C*

JOHN WARRACK

Good performances of Schubert's C major symphony are not hard to find on records; great ones are rare, and some of the few really great ones are no longer available in the lists, though eventually they may come back as 'historic'. Toscanini's 1941 performance (which is available) is certainly historic: it has some beautifully lyrical playing in it, though it is also rather hard driven, and the recording is rough. Another historic recording is Furtwängler's, a noble performance in his most powerful vein, slow and perhaps rather massive for the work's poignant lyricism, but filled with a true sense of symphonic growth that is often missing from younger conductors' versions. Klemperer's performance has been deleted but has yet to have earned the title 'historic', which it certainly should do, for here was one of the most powerful and penetrating of all performances of the work. Meanwhile, of the senior generation there remains Boult, master of a work he has always understood and loved, and Böhm, another artist who has grown old in affection for it; and we also have a pair of performances by the late Josef Krips.

There is no shortage of younger conductors eager to record the symphony either, and the most rewarding of the senior to middle generation are Giulini and Haitink, together with the late Istvan Kertesz. No one in his twenties, Schubert's own age when he wrote the symphony, has made a recording to set beside these in quality; and as so often with Schubert, it seems to be great length of experience that brings understanding of how to hold in the balance of this huge structure the lyrical intensity and the sense of bright energy against a knowledge of darkness. Josef Krips, for example, in the second of his two recordings with the London Symphony Orchestra (Decca), opens the work gently and affectionately, and with the sense of a long journey begun. Warm and sympathetic as the playing is, it tends to underestimate the originality of the horn opening, and all that is initiated by it. It is an eight-bar phrase, traditionally enough, but it is divided up into three, three, and two, and much of the metric tension in the symphony arises from this pull between the four-square and the unexpected rearrangement of it. Bernard Haitink, with the Concertgebouw Orchestra, opens with a rather stronger emphasis on how a two-bar horn phrase is given a one-bar answer, then the same again, and finally a two-bar answer to the whole melody. This kind of subtle attention to phrasing serves to make it more than a tune or a fanfare, but a proper opening to a complex symphonic experience, especially when Haitink balances it so well with the woodwind answer and then the rich string counterpoint.

In very different vein is one of the newest versions, by Giulini with the Chicago Symphony, which takes another view of the ambiguous marking, Andante. However sensitive and alert to nuances, it is the speed which is the real surprise; but the surprises are only just beginning. Before returning to his performance, I must refer to one of the greatest of all interpreters of the symphony, Sir Adrian Boult, with the LPO. His sense of movement forward from the Andante into the Allegro non troppo is very classically handled, with the traditional interpretation of the tempo change as the Allegro being more than twice the speed of the Andante, so that there is a stepping up of pace, and with it of mood, into the Allegro. Giulini, on the other hand, is unique in refusing to accept this tempo change. Indeed, he not only regards the tempo as constant, but, arising from that, the dotted rhythms and their phrasing as moving unaltered from Andante into Allegro, demanding not vigorous re-emphasis in the new context but the same kind of broad lyrical sweep.

Yet Giulini's is a remarkable new reading of the work, and one which it must be said he sustains with the greatest musicianship and insight. Whether it can be justified or not is a question of performance, not scholarship: I did consult Dr Ernst Hilmar, who has the bulk of Schubert's sketches in his care in the National Library in Vienna and is the leading expert on them, and he tells me that there is no known documentary evidence for Giulini's stance. But the question is, can it be justified musically? For much of the time, Giulini's extraordinary qualities of intensity and control bring it off; but there are sacrifices. The speed of the very opening seems excessive; and by regarding the tempo as constant, Giulini is unable to relax the rather measured pace he then has to take for the Allegro when he comes to the second subject, which in his handling is a little ponderous. Not that there is any need to slow up for this tune, as Furtwängler does, convincingly in his own terms; Istvan Kertesz, with the Vienna Philharmonic Orchestra, for instance, hardly yields at all in actual tempo, at the same time giving the tune a nice sense of relaxation. His is a fairly straightforward, well-shaped performance in traditional vein with players who have long had the music in their blood. Karl Böhm, with the Berlin Philharmonic, is more emphatic with the horn opening, which he takes at quite a slow tempo, then stepping up the pace for the change into the Allegro and thus giving himself room for manoeuvre into a slower tempo for the second subject.

When we come to the second movement, we again encounter this problematic tempo marking Andante, in this case with the rider, 'con moto'. Krips plays it in a pleasantly straightforward manner, the string quavers supporting warm, gentle, even rather rueful playing of the oboe tune. Yet, as Sir Adrian Boult suggests, the music is not really pleasant at all: the steadily marching strings are in the pace and the vein of Schubert's *Wanderer*, a figure that haunted him all his brief life; and the oboe melody is touching for its sense of jauntiness in the face of darkness. Boult's sense of darkness is justified when we come to the extraordinary heart of this movement. Istvan Kertesz plays it lucidly and firmly, but says too little about the power and the sense of crisis that comes over the music. The point is not missed by Giulini; but the breadth and the lyricism which led him to make his deductions about the opening movement now commit him to an intensification of the warmth, and this leads him into exaggerating the phrasing beyond what it can possibly take.

His passionate answer to the climax, sixteen bars before the A major section, is surely of a nature that belongs to a later phase of Romanticism; and it sounds sentimental, because it merely applies warmth to what is one of the most terrifying moments in all Schubert. The music has steadily increased in tension, until it is torn apart on a grinding sequence of diminished sevenths; in the stunned silence in the wake of this crisis and disintegration, the cello tune is an attempt at consolation, but its repeated phrases have a striving, still unresolved quality, and peace is not really reached until the music achieves the major key. This is a terrible, marvellous passage, and, apart from Klemperer, it is Bernard Haitink who responds most fully to it.

The Scherzo is marked Allegro vivace, and Giulini is sensitive to the Allegro but not really to the vivace; nor is he alone in this, for other conductors, including Böhm, suggest that the dance at the back of the invention is not so much the minuet as a stamping Ländler. Böhm reinforces his approach to the movement as one of considerable weight by emphasizing the thickness of the wind and brass scoring, and certainly he makes more of it than Krips, with his easy charm, though Krips does manage the turn into the Trio delightfully. However, that these demands are not irreconcilable is shown by Boult, whose mastery of structure is superbly displayed across the vast span of the first movement and the Finale, but is equally excellent in the way he relates the vigour of the Scherzo to the lighter dance movement of the Trio. Sir Adrian Boult, incidentally, takes the repeat of the Scherzo. Again, Bernard Haitink shows that there is no need to lose the sense of strength in order to do full justice to the lyrical charm of the music; like Boult, he has a true grasp on the structure of the music, and perhaps his gifts as a Bruckner conductor find expression in this work which stands as such a crucial ancestor to Bruckner's symphonies.

So to the Finale, a movement which can for the player be insufferably tedious or truly thrilling. Boult's lofty control, Krips's engaging delight in detail, Kertesz's energy and clarity, Böhm's strength – all have their point, though the most original and exciting plunge into the music seems to me to come from Giulini. But, exhilarating as Giulini is at the start of the movement, and brilliant as his playing of it remains, there is too much to question in his performance for it really to become one's first choice for a performance to live with: his odd relationship between the introduction and the main part of the first movement, his effusiveness in the Andante, other points which are consistent within his performance, but which seem to conflict with the nature of the symphony. Krips, on the other hand, is almost too easy about it all, attractive as much of his performance is; and Kertesz can for other reasons seem to move too readily across passages that are crucial to the complexity and richness and darkness of the work. Böhm is more serious, and there is much to admire in his dark but still imposing and warm view of the work; and Boult remains one of the symphony's great conductors, in his eighties still master of its huge arching spans and its subtleties of detail. Deeply as I admire this wise, penetrating performance, I think Haitink's has still more to offer, in its feeling for the sense of crisis and despair which lies at the back of much of the music, giving the brightness and energy a more moving quality. Of all the performances currently on record, the best of them offering different and valid kinds of insight, it is Haitink's which responds most fully to all that the music contains.

Recordings Discussed

Philadelphia Orchestra/Toscanini	RCA AT 102 (mono)
Berlin Philharmonic Orchestra/Furtwängler	Deutsche Grammophon 2535 808
Concertgebouw Orchestra/Krips	Decca ECS 714
London Symphony Orchestra/Krips	Decca SPA 467
Berlin Philharmonic Orchestra/Böhm	Deutsche Grammophon 138 877
Vienna Philharmonic Orchestra/Kertesz	Decca SXL 6089
London Philharmonic Orchestra/Boult	HMV ASD 2856
*Concertgebouw Orchestra/Haitink	Philips 9500 097
Chicago Symphony Orchestra/Giulini	Deutsche Grammophon 2530 882

© John Warrack

Stravinsky   *The Firebird*

NOËL GOODWIN

The Firebird was the first of the three famous ballets that brought Stravinsky an international reputation in the years before 1914, the others being *Petrushka* and *The Rite of Spring*. He was twenty-seven years old when Sergey Diaghilev heard his first major orchestral piece, *Fireworks*, at St Petersburg in 1909, and on the strength of it invited the composer to write the music for a projected ballet on the Firebird legend. Stravinsky was at first reluctant, partly because he was not then certain of his capabilities, and partly because, as he later put it, 'It demanded descriptive music of a kind I did not want to write'.

Fortunately for him, however, he accepted the commission, and in a none-too-cordial collaboration with Mikhail Fokin as choreographer achieved one of the most successful of all the ballets presented by the Diaghilev company. It was first performed at the Paris Opéra on 25 June 1910, with Tamara Karsavina as the Firebird, and Fokin himself as Prince Ivan. Gabriel Pierné conducted. Its immediate success made Stravinsky a celebrity, and the ballet is still performed the world over, both in its original choreography as the Royal Ballet does, and in other versions.

Stravinsky dedicated his score to his friend and teacher Rimsky-Korsakov, and it remained the music by which he became best known to the wider public. Indeed, it became so closely associated with him that, as he later related, he was once addressed, quite seriously in public, as 'Mr. Fireberg'. Stravinsky tended to deprecate the work in later years as not very original, on account of the folk music element in it, but in fact this helps the pictorial aspect as the human characters – Ivan and the Princesses – have diatonic folk melodies, while the supernatural ones – the Firebird and the evil sorcerer Kashchey – are presented in chromatic music based on the interval of a tritone.

I am not concerning myself here with the short concert suites that Stravinsky later made, but with the full score in its original lavish orchestration: at present there are six records of this available. One is conducted by Stravinsky, in a bright, well-focused performance by the Columbia Symphony Orchestra. Although the record first came out here all of seventeen years ago, it is now reissued as part of an album with all three of Stravinsky's early ballets in it. It still sounds fresh and clear, and the performance gives us an instructive point of reference for the composer's own intentions towards the work. A more recent record, issued in 1977, is conducted by Antal Dorati, who seems to me to take a rather charmless view, for example, of the scene in the enchanted garden at the beginning of the ballet, where the composer is much more effective. Although Dorati (with the Royal Philharmonic Orchestra) is the most recent record, I did not warm very much to the character of it in the opening scenes. Partly this is due to the recording, which gives a close focus of individual instruments without a balancing sense of perspective, so that the enchanted garden lacks the ambience of mystery and magic. Dorati is an experienced man of the theatre, of course, but oddly enough it is Pierre Boulez (who has never, I think, conducted *The Firebird* in the theatre) who presents the scene in more magically seductive colours with the New York Philharmonic. This is often a fascinating performance, chiefly in the way in which he blends or contrasts the individual strands in the orchestral texture. You have only to read through the score to see with what skill and sublety Stravinsky marked his phrasing and dynamics on line after line, and it is this to which Boulez gives his closest attention. Yet, if he had any experience of the work in the theatre I do not think he would be so cavalier in his treatment of tempo. His waltz for the Firebird's dance is somewhat breathless and I am quite sure that no ballerina would attempt the Firebird's first solo at the speed Boulez takes it, a speed which is also markedly faster than Stravinsky's own tempo indication. Nor is this the only instance of Boulez varying the speed very considerably from what the score suggests. A little later in this opening scene, for instance, he whips up the tempo for the dance of the princesses with their golden apples, so that it sounds almost competitive instead of just playful, whereas the fanfares right at the end of the ballet are so slow as to sound merely pompous instead of radiant.

To return to the Firebird's Dance, the counterbalance to the rather breathless haste of the Boulez performance is provided by Bernard Haitink conducting the London Philharmonic Orchestra. On the whole Haitink's performance of the Firebird's Dance seems to me closer than Boulez to its choreographic character, and also to its musical intentions. The main difference between Haitink and Stravinsky's own performance is in the way that the composer communicates more liveliness of spirit within the slower basic speed. And this, I think, is the advantage for those conductors who have conducted the ballet in the theatre. This tells even more strongly against Haitink in a passage which, unlike the Firebird's Dance and the other best-known passages such as the Princesses' Dance, the Infernal Dance, and the Lullaby, does not occur in the familiar concert suite. Immediately after the Firebird's Dance, she is pursued and caught by Ivan. She struggles in vain as he holds her fast, and then submits in a sad phrase on the solo viola. In spite of the fact that Haitink is entirely faithful to the score here, and directs with absolute accuracy so far as the orchestra is concerned, to me it does not convey the dramatic character of the scene –

Ivan's excitement and eagerness in chasing the Firebird, her despair at being captured by him, the fierceness of her struggles at first, and then her pathos at realizing these are in vain. All this, though, is communicated, for instance, in Stravinsky's own performance.

From this point in the ballet the captive Firebird pleads with Prince Ivan for her release, and obtains it by giving him one of her feathers, as a token of her promise to come to his assistance, should he be in danger and call on her with the feather. Ivan's next encounter is with the princesses – thirteen of them, according to the story – who are captive to Kaschey. They are all beautiful, of course, with one just that bit more beautiful than the others, and before falling in love with this one, Ivan watches them in a game with golden apples plucked from a tree in the enchanted garden. This is given a cheerful spirit in Dorati's performance apart from the abrupt ending to Side 1. Technically it may be a useful spot, because it reaches a silent bar, but musically it is far from satisfactory. *The Firebird* in its complete form lasts around forty-five minutes, so it has to have a turnover, and my six records between them put it in three different places – two in each. Dorati shares the same unsatisfactory moment with Haitink. In the older of Ansermet's two performances, he continues through the Princesses' meeting with Ivan to their graceful Round Dance, after Ivan declares his love, and ends the side much more effectively at that magical moment before trumpets herald the break of day.

Ansermet conducts the Suisse Romande Orchestra, and the recording, which first came out just twenty-one years ago, was reissued in 1977 on a reduced-price label. At the moment it has the cheaper price range to itself, and although the performance detail is less clear than later recordings, with a subdued level and narrower range of dynamics, the style of the performance is theatrically expressive and musically still quite acceptable. The same turnover point is shared by the Boulez performance, which enables the second side of his record to start with a vivid Daybreak Scene, making effective use of stereo separation and distance in the trumpet calls.

The second of Ansermet's records and Stravinsky's own make their turnover just before Kashchey's entourage of grotesque monsters erupt on to the scene. Ansermet brings a splendidly menacing character to this passage – so much a precursor of *The Rite of Spring* – in the later of his two performances. It was made with the New Philharmonia Orchestra during a visit to London not long before he died. There is, in fact, a great deal to enjoy in this Ansermet performance, which first came out in 1970. It has an eloquent feeling for both the musical and choreographic character of the work; the orchestral playing is of a high standard, and the recording balance combines richness with clarity. The record is part of a two-disc album in which the second record (free of charge) is made from Ansermet's rehearsal sessions with the orchestra, with his spoken comments in English on various fragmented passages of the music in equally fragmented English. No doubt this is fascinating to the student, whether of Stravinsky or of conducting, but Ansermet's older and cheaper performance still sounds by no means outclassed. The playing of the Suisse Romande Orchestra is responsive and filled with character; it has a sense of grace and mystery in the earlier scenes, and a vigorous spirit in the dances with Kashchey and his monsters. In terms of value for money it is worth keeping in mind as a cheaper alternative – in fact, the only cheaper alternative – to the other versions, which are all at full price.

This includes Stravinsky's own performance, which is only four years younger than Ansermet's, but which has a brighter quality of sound and a splendidly sinister urgency, for example, in the Infernal Dance. The drawback to this record is that it is no longer available on its own, but only as part of a three-disc album at full price, which also has his performances of *Petrushka* and *The Rite of Spring*. I would have thought that performances as old as these ought to be available at a reduced price by now, but I am told that this cannot be because the album is still at full price in other EEC countries. In many other Stravinsky works the composer's performances have been outclassed by others, but there is no doubt in my mind that his record of *The Firebird* is ideally the one to have and, if you can afford the investment, the other two discs in the album are also worth having. The best alternative record on its own at full price is Boulez with the New York Philharmonic, in spite of my reservations about his choice of tempos; or there is Ansermet's reduced-price alternative.

Recordings Discussed

*Columbia Symphony Orchestra/Stravinsky	CBS S 78046 (part of 3-record set)
*Suisse Romande Orchestra/Ansermet	Decca ECS 817
New Philharmonia Orchestra/Ansermet	Decca SET 468
London Philharmonic Orchestra/Haitink	Philips 6500 483
*New York Philharmonic Orchestra/Boulez	CBS 76418
Royal Philharmonic Orchestra/Dorati	Enigma 53534

© Noël Goodwin

Vaughan Williams *'A London Symphony'* *(Symphony No. 2)*

MICHAEL KENNEDY

The earliest of the six available recordings was made in 1952, the latest in 1978, and each is a very good performance, well recorded. Probably many listeners learnt the work, as I did, from the old Decca 78 set made by Sir Henry Wood and the Queen's Hall Orchestra in the 1930s, a now historic performance. Before that there was a version by Sir Dan Godfrey and the Bournemouth Municipal Orchestra. Only four conductors are represented in the versions now under review because both Sir Adrian Boult and Sir John Barbirolli recorded the symphony twice. The other two performances are conducted by André Previn, a record issued in 1972, and by Vernon Handley, who recorded it for Classics for Pleasure, the most recent.

Although the performance of music is not something to be judged by stop-watch timings, tempo fluctuation plays such a large part in the interpretation of 'A London Symphony' that it is interesting to note that there is nearly five minutes' difference between the shortest performance, which is Boult's second recording, made in 1971, and the longest, Barbirolli's second, made in 1967. Both of these dedicated Vaughan Williams interpreters add over a minute to the first movement in their second recordings and, more surprisingly, both take the slow movement faster the second time, Boult by as much as a minute and a half.

Although the 'London Symphony' has illustrative features, it is not a programme symphony. Sonata-form structure underpins the whole work, which is an impressionist musical portrait of the city, much as Debussy's *La Mer* is of the sea. In fact there is a lot of Debussy's influence in the music, and the symphony begins in a very similar way to *La Mer*, with a quiet atmospheric introduction. This surely represents the city asleep, as in Wordsworth's famous sonnet, and just how effective a performance will be can and must be established at the start by the playing of these slow arching phrases by strings, horns, and woodwind. Each phrase has a comma after it which the composer says must be taken as a breath-mark, not as a pause. Vernon Handley, with the London Philharmonic Orchestra, perhaps makes these catches of the breath pretty nearly into pauses, but he draws a very atmospheric picture of dawn, with a feeling of veiled mystery. This is a tribute to the tone-colour from the London Philharmonic Orchestra violas and cellos and the excellent blending of wind and strings.

The introduction ends with the first of the work's several picturesque touches, the half-hour striking at Westminster. This is scored for harp and clarinet, with harmonies on the horns; and it is the signal for the city to wake from its slumbers, with a crescendo from the woodwind section leading into the harsh and forceful first subject. Previn is pre-eminent here in letting both harp and clarinet be heard in the chimes and in obtaining a really rasping snarl from the brass after the first statement of the main theme to go with the strings' *sul ponticello*. Care for detail and exuberance distinguish the whole of their recording.

A difficult section in the first movement comes with what one could call the Hampstead-Heath-on-Bank-Holiday episode, but is really the second-subject group of themes. Woodwind and brass have a kind of fanfare which is followed by a very chirpy little tune for the strings. The woodwind, not to be outdone, contribute another merry snippet. The strings' tune is quite a test for the players; the second note in each bar is a semi-quaver and this is often overlooked in the anxiety to obtain good spiccato playing and not to play too loud. But if done correctly the tune is given just that extra little bit of Cockney humour. Barbirolli, expert that he was in training string players, was particularly successful (in his first, 1957, Hallé recording) in this section, where the composer imparted a bright gleam to the brass by his use of cornets in addition to trumpets.

The first Hallé recording, though not my first choice, is nevertheless a special favourite of mine, and it has been reissued in Pye's Collector series at a very reasonable price. The recording is much brighter and captures more detail than Boult's first version, and the interpretation is very full of character. It was made in December 1957 at a time when the Hallé and Barbirolli were playing a lot of Vaughan Williams, who admired their performances very much. It was to Barbirolli that Vaughan Williams confessed that the 'London' was his own favourite among his symphonies, and he also told me that, in his old age, he envied the richness of sound he had put into this work forty years earlier. The Hallé gave a memorable performance of this symphony with the composer in the audience at the Cheltenham Festival in July 1958, about five weeks before Vaughan Williams died, and this recording comes very close to what was heard on that unforgettable occasion. Barbirolli and the Hallé are especially effective in the most lyrical episode of the first movement, when two solo cellos, two solo violins and the harp introduce the first moments of relief from the bustle and noise of London, with the impression of a park, or perhaps a church, and what almost seems like a reminiscence in the strings of the Tallis Fantasia.

I have twice used the word 'episode' to describe passages in the symphony, but I must not give the impression that this is an episodic movement or even an episodic symphony. True, it is almost embarrassed by the amount of material, but this is held together by real symphonic tensions so that even a quiet passage like the one I have just referred to, and which takes the risk of bringing the movement to a standstill at its central point, is completely convincing in its context, quite apart from being beautiful anyway. No conductor has a surer grasp of the strictly symphonic logic and construction of this symphony than André Previn who, with the London Symphony Orchestra, draws together all the threads of the first movement in the coda. When the theme broadens out on the full orchestra he is completely accurate in increasing the volume, as the score requires, from *fff* to *ffff* and gives full rein to the strident climax.

One of the criticisms still sometimes levelled at Vaughan Williams is that he was technically inept in handling the orchestra. He made several self-deprecatory remarks to that effect which unfortunately have been taken seriously. But the truth is that he was a masterly orchestrator, and in one particular way above all others. He scored his music so that it sounds like Vaughan Williams and no one else. He knew just what he wanted and how to get it. The 'London' Symphony is full of poetic and felicitous scoring, particularly for woodwind and solo strings, and for sheer creation of a mood the slow movement is unequalled in this respect. Vaughan Williams describes it as 'Bloomsbury Square on a November Afternoon'. There is an autumnal dankness in the air, a suggestion that it might turn foggy. Through the gloom we hear the jingle of a hansom cab – for this is the London of 1910 – and a lavender-seller cries her wares. The conductor must give his orchestral soloists here a recitative-like freedom and yet must not let the tempo become self-indulgent, because he very soon has to screw up the tension and release it again in a great gush of romantic fervour. Barbirolli and the Hallé in their first recording revel in this passage, where Sydney Errington's viola solo has a mellowness of tone which is not approached on any of the other recordings. The woodwind soloists' phrasing is also expressively moulded and Barbirolli, himself a Londoner, who knew these Edwardian squares in his childhood, is in his element when it comes to those sinister bars for brass marked *misterioso*. But Barbirolli's intensity of 1957 is matched by Sir Adrian Boult's 1971 performance, made when he was eighty-two but full of the ardour of youth. Boult first conducted this symphony in 1918 and he is the only conductor still alive who conducted the original version before the composer cut it and made other revisions. His knowledge of it is therefore not only profound but unrivalled, and it is obvious that it has never lost its appeal for him. His earlier performance, made in 1952, is vivid but less well recorded than Barbirolli's first version and much less well than his own second one. In the later recording, the climax of the slow movement combines grandeur and human passion in a remarkable way, and shows how well the recording engineers have captured the widely separated ranges of upper and lower strings. There is a temptation to speed up the tempo at this point but Boult keeps it absolutely steady.

The most original movement is the Scherzo which the composer subtitled 'Nocturne'. Flaring lights, street musicians, and that sense of loneliness in a big city which pervades the whole work – all these are in this Scherzo, which is the trickiest movement to play and to interpret. *Allegro vivace* is the marking at the start, and the strings are muted. They must sound springy and pliable, with a very taut rhythm, and they must play *pianissimo*; and here I find Vernon Handley and the London Philharmonic Orchestra set a fine standard. Previn adopts much the same tempo but there is a brighter tone to the strings which slightly detracts from the nocturnal mood. Yet neither he nor Handley quite achieves Boult's lightness of touch later in the movement when the scoring is heavier. This is entirely a matter of rhythm, and the London Philharmonic Orchestra give Boult superbly tensile playing in his second recording. In Barbirolli's second record, made for HMV in 1967, the performance of the Scherzo differs considerably from his version of ten years earlier. The tempo is much slower and is certainly not *allegro vivace*. Yet Barbirolli obviously thought deeply about this, and the change of speed is no mere quirky decision. Paradoxically there is a strengthening of the rhythm, and although I cannot feel that the tempo is right, it certainly reveals the music's basic strength. Later in the movement there is a famous passage where strings and muted horns imitate an accordeon as introduction to a lusty chorus of street music, the kind of injection of popular music into a symphony which Mahler accomplished with Viennese material, though the influence here was very obviously Stravinsky's *Petrushka*. Barbirolli adopts a somewhat eccentric tempo, with the joviality suppressed but with the rhythmical pulse strongly defined. In contrast to this very romantic approach Previn is much more exuberant, backed up by very precise and razor-sharp playing by the London Symphony Orchestra. Previn also insists on absolutely accurate note values from the side-drummer.

The Finale also poses a problem of tempo. Its main theme is a march and Vaughan Williams asks for a tempo 'quasi lento'. Is it a funeral march or a ceremonial procession or, as was suggested at one time, a hunger march? Barbirolli's second version is definitely funereal. But this is structurally the weakest movement of the symphony and Barbirolli's expansive treatment is surely too indulgent and tends to emphasize this rather than to conceal it, for all his commitment to the music. It is here that Boult triumphs over all rivals, including Previn, and it is his interpretation of the Finale which clinches his 1971 performance and makes it, for me, the first choice of the six now in the catalogue, though if I could afford only a lower-priced record I would go for Barbirolli's 1957 version.

Boult's performance, so well played by the London Philharmonic, has all Barbirolli's intensity and romantic fervour, all Previn's structural control and brilliance of detail, and all Handley's level-headed judgement of tempos; but it also has that indefinable but easily recognizable authority which comes from long association with the score and its composer. One feels, listening to Boult, that he has long ago solved the work's musical problems and is now able to communicate the composer's vision almost as if he had composed it himself. Nowhere is this more in evidence than in the Finale, where he drives the symphony to its ecstatic climax with a sureness of purpose no one else quite achieves, and the London Philharmonic Orchestra trombones make a really noble sound, with time to articulate every note. 'With all its faults I love it still', Vaughan Williams said of this symphony, and it is obvious from their performance that Boult and the London Philharmonic Orchestra feel the same.

Recordings Discussed

London Philharmonic Orchestra/Boult (1952)	Decca ECS 616
*Hallé Orchestra/Barbirolli (1957)	Pye GSGC 14012
Hallé Orchestra/Barbirolli (1969)	HMV SXLP 30180
*London Philharmonic Orchestra/Boult (1971)	HMV ASD 2740
London Symphony Orchestra/Previn	RCA SB 6860
London Philharmonic Orchestra/Handley	CFP 40286

© Michael Kennedy

Vivaldi   *The Four Seasons*

STEPHEN DODGSON

Baroque composers, like bakers, were accustomed to provide sonatas and concertos by the dozen. So it was with the *Four Seasons*, heading Vivaldi's Op.8 which consists of twelve concertos in all. And I think it is worth keeping in mind the title which Vivaldi gave to the set as a whole: *The Trial of Harmony and Invention*, clear testimony of the vivid effect he believed his music would make.

To keep this review within manageable proportions, I have concentrated on ten versions only. The fourteen versions which I have been obliged to omit would easily make a review in themselves, with such illustrious names among violinists as Suk, Perlman, and Szeryng, and, amongst conductors, Stokowski and Karajan. With style unavoidably a prime reason for making this initial selection, I feel I should begin by showing where my own stylistic responses lie. This happens to be well illustrated by one version which outwardly looks particularly promising; it is by I Solisti Veneti directed by Claudio Scimone, well known specialist in the music of Vivaldi, a fellow Venetian. In the opening 'Danza Pastorale' from *Spring*, Scimone takes a faster tempo than is actually needed to evoke the arcadian charm of the scene, with nymphs, shepherds, and a bagpipe. But the fact that he quite misses its two most beautiful ingredients – innocent melody and graceful movement – is due to a taste for a heavy luxurious tone coupled with swimmy phrasing. Schneiderhahn, soloist with the Lucerne Festival Strings, at the same rather fast speed, shows just what Scimone misses – a revealing transparency to match a dance in the Spring sunshine. Everything is finely poised and delicate in articulation and tone. But all too often unaccountably fast.

Notably steady throughout a long association with Vivaldi and his *Seasons* has been Karl Münchinger and the Stuttgart Chamber Orchestra – the very best of whose three versions was the first, unfortunately no longer available. It seems a case of progressing backwards, for, of the two Stuttgart versions currently available from Decca, the best is emphatically the older, cheaper one, in which Werner Krotzinger is the soloist: this is a reliable bargain version in Decca's popular 'World of the Great Classics' series, yet it is a little too ponderous and German for such a very Italian landscape. In this respect I believe there are three other cheap versions which surpass it, and one of them with particular ease: the recording from Saga in which the solo violinist is Giuliano Badini, with the Sinfonia di Siena. I know nothing of either soloist or orchestra, but this record is the one which, more than any other, that I kept coming back to.

Spring gives way to *Summer* and is not the best of seasons in Italy according to Vivaldi's programme, because of its overpowering heat, tormenting insects, violent storms. However, before things get too bad, at the first solo passage in the concerto, there is one of the most enchanting cuckoos in all music, soon followed by a lovesick turtle dove and the lofty trills of a goldfinch. There is a beautiful ease and accuracy to this catalogue of birds from Zukerman, with sonorous, vital playing by the English Chamber Orchestra in support. Of all the starry names amongst violin virtuosos, Zukerman seems to me the most sensitive to the music's scale, and secures an elegant supporting performance from the orchestra, marred only by a continuo player determined to have his own Trial of Harmony and Invention with the composer! And several versions, specially the English ones, are also rather like this.

In Russia, harpsichordists are evidently not permitted such freedom, if a rather fascinating Russian record of *The Seasons* is anything to go by. The soloist with the Leningrad Philharmonic Chamber Orchestra is Mikhail Vaiman, whose finesse and artistry are of a class with Zukerman. All the string playing is distinguished in this well-recorded account, and the only disappointment is the rather weak portrayal of the baroque concerto as such.

The record by Collegium Aureum on original instruments, with the violinist Franzjosef Maier, carefully handles tonal weight and has an excellent recorded sound to match. It might seem a likely contender in anyone's choice, specially for those with a keen historic sense. Unexpectedly, however, the musical pursuit is not authenticity of style, but a much more romantic view of the concertos, enormously elaborate in detail and very wayward in tempo. With all possible (and a few impossible) opportunities to sigh and languish avidly seized upon, the whole effect is rather enervating. There is, incidentally, one other unexpected thing: the performance is at modern pitch. But a concern for baroque style is very evident in performances by the Academy of St Martin-in-the-Fields on Argo, and by the English Concert on CRD.

After the warbling goldfinch, a threatening wind; but it soon vanishes, and the oppressive heat returns, with the soloist painting a touching picture of a peasant weeping for his crops about to be laid low. Alan Loveday treats this with a discreet tenderness, which his colleagues in the Academy match with a generally rather more fulsome sweetness. Amid the rapidly changing moods, Simon Preston, busy harpsichordist during the winds, is suddenly revealed at a rather prettily-toned little organ for the plaintive peasant. Infectious energy for the fast sections, contrasted with maximum prettiness in the slow sections is very much the character of the Academy in these concertos.

To a degree, so it is with the English Concert, inclining to exaggerate both fast and slow tempos. Another likeness is the speed with which Trevor Pinnock likewise moves from harpsichord to organ – and for just the same motives. But what makes the English Concert quite distinct is their use of actual and reproduction eighteenth-century instruments and (unlike Collegium Aureum) the low pitch that goes with them. Their soloist, Simon Standage, is recorded rather close, so as to compensate, I imagine, for the lighter sound of his baroque violin, but this does here and there give a rather nasal edginess to his tone.

Autumn is the season of Bacchus, and some spectacular lurching effects are required from the soloist in the first movement between appearances of the dancing ritornello of the harvesters. One of the most successful of the older versions of *The Seasons* is by the polished Italian group, I Musici, with Roberto Michelucci as soloist. I find I Musici just a little too deliberate in much of this music: it makes them sound somehow a little old-fashioned. Or is this sensation due to Roberto Michelucci, rather prone to hesitations even when not portraying a drunk?

Another definitely worthwhile bargain version of *The Seasons* is played by the Virtuosi of England; moreover their soloist, Kenneth Sillito, is particularly good, and it is his contribution to this bargain 'Classic for Pleasure' which makes it tempting. The Virtuosi of England under Arthur Davison are reliable, though a good deal less subtle.

The English Concert have several moments when they skilfully combine an ornamental baroque rhetoric with pictorial ideas, such as the gradual saturation with liquor until sleep is the only remedy. Specially noteworthy in this version I think is the playing of the cello continuo. From him above all springs the conviction that this is true baroque playing. Giuliano Badini and the Sinfonia di Siena, are generally much less complex in interpretation. And, paradoxically, their sleep seems to me more completely sleepy even though it moves a great deal more.

I want now to offer a few thoughts concerning Vivaldi's slow movements as seen in my selection of available versions of *The Seasons*. They are all miniature movements, and look nothing on paper; yet how captivating their effect when tempo, texture, and melodic line exactly touch off the feeling of a perfect floating stillness. Three versions narrowly miss this, one achieves it completely. In the slow movement of *Spring* (which describes a goatherd asleep, with his dog supplying a friendly growl faithfully once a bar on the violas), Alan Loveday, with the Academy of St. Martin-in-the-Fields, has a most delicate tenderness for the melody which almost disguises the fact that the tempo is too slow. Schneiderhahn, on the other hand, seems quite unnecessarily brisk. Yet what is remarkable about Schneiderhahn's Deutsche Grammophon Privilege version is that although his slow movements are all much too fast, he does still achieve a feeling of serenity – and that I take as an indication of his distinction. A version of this movement that seems just right is Pinchas Zukerman's full-priced record with the English Chamber Orchestra on CBS. Yet, the serenity is less than with Schneiderhahn because Zukerman applies a richer expressive contour and shading to the solo line. The only other full-price version I really think worthwhile considering is the CRD issue of the English Concert, but it does have some rather exaggerated tempos, and I personally tire of the rather nasal sound, as recorded, of the solo violin.

Among the less than full-priced issues, there is more choice, and the possibilities are more tempting. Sillito on Classics for Pleasure, is cheapest of all. Schneiderhan offers delicacy and finesse, if you don't mind his fast speeds. Then there is the interesting Russian performance on mid-priced HMV 'Concert Classics'; or Münchinger and the Stuttgart Chamber Orchestra, a shade solid and unimaginative, on Decca's cheapest label. These could all be reasonable choices, but the Saga issue of the Sinfonia di Siena directed by its soloist, Giuliano Badini, surpasses them all– and all the full-priced ones too. And the way all four slow movements succeed clinches the matter as I see it, and at its price it is a bargain disc. But I ought perhaps to advise getting out a magnifying glass before purchase, since the one I listened to invariably had to be helped over a couple of repeating grooves.

Recordings Discussed

Krotzinger/Stuttgart Chamber Orchestra/ Münchinger	Decca SPA 201
Schneiderhan/Lucerne Festival Strings/Baumgartner	Deutsche Grammophon 135 024
Loveday/Academy of St Martin-in-the-Fields/ Marriner	Argo ZRG 654
Michelucci/I Musici	Philips 6500 017
Toso/I Solisti Veneti/Scimone	Erato STU 70679
Zukerman/English Chamber Orchestra	CBS 73097
Sillito/Virtuosi of England/Davison	CFP 40016
Kulka/Stuttgart Chamber Orchestra/Münchinger	Decca SXL 6557
Vaiman/Leningrad Philharmonic Chamber Orchestra/Shinder	HMV SXLP 30195
Standage/English Concert	CRD 1025
*Badini/Sinfonia di Siena	Saga 5443
Maier/Collegium Aureum	HM IC 065. 99666Q

© Stephen Dodgson

Franck   *Symphonic Variations*

DAVID MURRAY

For a work that seems as transparent as César Franck's Symphonic Variations, there is extraordinary disagreement about just what it offers variations of. According to the sleeve-note, you read that Franck was operating with one theme, or two, or three – and those that say 'three' disagree about which they are! – with or without introducing some 'new' themes along the way; furthermore, the piece is in either two or three parts. There is no agreement about how many variations there are, either, nor even where they start.

All this confusion is a tribute to Franck's ingenuity, and to his not being German. If a proper set of variations has a proper main theme, which is duly apotheosized at the end, that is not what Franck wrote. What I call the theme – which the composer asked to be played 'expressively and with simplicity' – appears about a third of the way through, at the hundredth bar. It is followed by 170 bars of varied repetitions, never venturing far from F sharp minor and major, and in one basic tempo – 'Allegretto quasi andante' – until the last, which is a sort of nocturne, marked 'much slower'. All that, which Tovey called a mere 'important episode in variation form', is preceded by a long introduction that recalls the slow movement of Beethoven's G major Concerto: stern strings in bare octaves, gently pleading piano.

Out of the orchestral suggestions, Franck constructs his variation-theme; the piano subject is to be saved until the last variation, and then transformed into the chief tune of the Finale. But first it needs to be properly planted, and piano and orchestra unite for the first time. The piano sketches a new idea, which the orchestra presses to a tentative climax; then strings and winds offer a first, join-the-dots version of the variation-theme; and the piano, alone, expands its original subject in high-Romantic style, *recitando*. Weissenberg, with the Berlin Philharmonic Orchestra under Karajan, is impeccable here: only a little slower than the basic *poco allegro,* just as Franck asks, and describing a clean curve up to the *appassionato* climax and down again. Other pianists are inclined to fuss with it; but it is not complicated enough for that – this is still the Introduction, after all – though it needs to be vivid. Marie-Françoise Bucquet's performance is scarcely that, and it is a pity that she is so tepid, and so rhythmically slack, for her programme is attractive: the Franck comes with D'Indy's Symphony on a French mountain song for piano and orchestra. and the Fauré Ballade. Franck wrote his Symphonic Variations in 1885, four years after the original solo version of the Ballade; he knew Fauré's work, and it might well have inspired the graceful intricacies of his own bigger piece.

Fauré's Ballade presents its first tune innocently at once. By the time the piano spells out Franck's variation-theme, it is already an intricate construction, with a genealogy behind it. Franck wanted it played 'con simplicità' nonetheless: we need the sense of settling firmly at last into the home key of F sharp minor, which has been held in suspension all through the Introduction. Unlike Curzon or Rogé, Weissenberg still sounds restless.

With the first variation, the dialogue between piano and orchestra becomes firmly fraternal; the introductory conflict has melted away, and the soloist's role appears in a different light. While the orchestra continues to revolve the theme – and both Karajan and Maazel (with Rogé) ensure that the orchestral voices carry – the piano executes a series of arabesques, or mini-études, very much in the manner of Schumann's Études Symphoniques for solo piano. Franck judged the balance to a nicety, keeping the piano mostly high and bright; but Curzon's Decca recording thrusts him into the foreground, leaving Boult and the London Philharmonic waving forlornly in the middle distance. The rest of Curzon's record, incidentally, is filled by the Grieg Concerto and the popular Litolff Scherzo, which may explain the glaring spotlight on the soloist. The main work on the Maazel-Rogé record is Franck's Symphony, and in the Symphonic Variations the piano is kept carefully in scale. It is worth noticing how seamlessly Rogé joins the third variation to the second, too. That is one of several points where Sylvia Kersenbaum, in her performance with Paavo Berglund and the Bournemouth Symphony, makes a small rip in the musical fabric; moreover she is recorded too loud.

Franck prescribed just one tempo for the whole chain of variations until the nocturne: a sudden surge sounds like a lurch. 'Allegretto quasi andante' means something like 'having the feeling of a slow variation-movement without actually being slow'. No one is as strict about that as Robert Casadesus, in his performance with Ormandy and the Philadelphia Orchestra. Even the theme is laid down briskly and plainly; Casadesus takes a very long and unsentimental view of the music. By comparison, in the exultant Lisztian variation Rogé sounds distressingly frantic – though he makes charming amends in the fifth variation, where Franck is obviously remembering Chopin's E flat Prelude. Like Rogé, Alicia de Larrocha flattens the dotted upbeats in the Lisztian variation into mere triplets, in her recording with the London Philharmonic under Rafael Frühbeck de Burgos; and at her tempo, the Chopinesque variation makes no mercurial contrast.

The last variation is what I call the 'nocturne', which Miss de Larrocha takes very slowly indeed. Franck marked it 'Molto piu lento' ('much slower', but perhaps not 'extremely slow'). Casadesus and Ormandy view it as a cello meditation, lightly frosted with piano arpeggios – which I happen to think is right – and they fix their tempo accordingly. Others choose to take it as at least as much a piano rêverie. Rogé's line is full of expressive little hesitations which seduce one's attention. In the second half of the variation, where Franck brings back the pathos-laden piano subject from the Introduction, Karajan contrives very deliberately to keep his strings a fraction behind Weissenberg's piano – as if each melody-note were touched off with bated breath by the piano. Curzon and Boult on the other hand strike a limpid balance.

There is more going on in the Finale than can really be heard in the Curzon-Boult recording. You can hear more of it in the new Supraphon performance by Ivan Moravec with Vaclav Neumann and the Czech Philharmonic – especially the brusque new cello version of the languishing piano-subject, which according to an old English musical joke says 'Get your hair cut!': an apt sentiment, given the famous *embourgeoisement* of the music at this point. But here Moravec is disappointingly un-brilliant with the figuration, and in general (as with the *con fuoco* piano passage just before it) the Czechs are inclined to ease themselves comfortably, and unstylishly, into passages that want sharper definition. Rogé's figuration glitters better; but then his treatment of the outrageously winsome second subject is somewhat mannered, where sheer un-selfconscious buoyancy is needed.

Collectors intent upon having up-to-date recorded sound may well choose the Rogé-Maazel version first. Attractive and alert, it suffers from nothing worse than a certain excess of personality over authority on the side of the soloist. The Weissenberg-Karajan performance is a close rival, though Weissenberg is over-restrained in the Finale. Curzon is inimitable, in his way, but too much of the orchestra's music can be heard only with the ear of faith. Elderly though the Casadesus-Ormandy recording is, it remains the one I should want. Casadesus's cool assurance does not stem the exuberant flow of the piece: quite the reverse.

Recordings Discussed

*Casadesus/Philadelphia Orchestra/Ormandy	CBS 61356
Curzon/London Philharmonic Orchestra/Boult	Decca SXL 2173
de Larrocha/London Philharmonic Orchestra/ Frühbeck	Decca SXL 6599
Weissenberg/Berlin Philharmonic Orchestra/ Karajan	HMV ASD 2872
Bucquet/National Opera Orchestra of Monte Carlo/Capolongo	Philips 6580 140
Kersenbaum/Bournemouth Symphony Orchestra/ Berglund	HMV ASD 3308

*Rogé/Cleveland Orchestra/Maazel

Moravec/Czech Philharmonic Orchestra/
   Neumann

Decca SXL 6823

Supraphon 4102073

© David Murray

Prokofiev   *Piano Concerto No. 3*

GEOFFREY NORRIS

Prokofiev was a formidable pianist, and in fact it was with a performance of his own First Piano Concerto, composed in 1911 and 1912, that he graduated from the St Petersburg Conservatory in 1914. The examiners on that occasion were divided as to the merits of Prokofiev's music; although he received praise from the younger element, Glazunov, then principal of the conservatory, found little to appeal to him in the concerto, and he was obliged to announce that Prokofiev had been successful in his exam in a 'flat, toneless mumble', as Prokofiev recalls in his autobiography. Despite Glazunov's disapproval, Prokofiev's future career as a pianist and composer was assured. Until the latter part of his life, when he retired from the concert platform, he was in constant demand as a soloist, specially during the decade or so when he lived outside Russia in the '20s. And he composed four more piano concertos, three of which were primarily intended for himself to perform. Nearly always, controversy surrounded the premières of these works. After he had played the complex Second Concerto for the first time in 1913, the critic of the principal St Petersburg newspaper commented that Prokofiev 'seemed to be either dusting the keys or striking high or low notes at random, with a sharp dry touch'. 'This music is enough to drive you mad', one couple were heard to remark as they made for the exit. Another verdict was that 'cats on a roof make better music'. The critic Karatygin made what turned out to be a much more sensible observation: 'The audience booed. This means nothing. Some ten years from now the same audience will pay for this booing with unanimous applause for what will then be a famous composer who will be recognized all over Europe.' Ten years later Prokofiev had indeed earned an international reputation, with several major works behind him, including the Classical Symphony, the First Violin Concerto, his Dostoyevsky opera *The Gambler* – and his Third Piano Concerto.

Not that the reception given to the Third Concerto was any more encouraging than his previous experiences of premières. A critic of the Chicago concert at which Prokofiev played the piece for the first time (on 16 December 1921) acknowledged the concerto tersely with the comment that it was 'greatly a matter of slewed harmony, neither conventional enough to win the affections nor modernist enough to be annoying'. When Prokofiev played it again in New York ten days later, the papers remarked that the concerto was 'singularly hard and dry as music, bringing little to nourish the intellect or warm the soul. It is difficult to imagine him being asked often to play it', the review continues, 'or any other pianist than Mr Prokofiev playing it.'

Yet the Third Concerto has surely entered the repertory as the most popular of all Prokofiev's piano concertos. (The Fourth, for the left hand, written specially for Paul Wittgenstein, has probably never really recovered from the damning note that Wittgenstein sent to Prokofiev on receiving the score: 'Thank you for your concerto, but I don't understand a single note, and shan't play it!' The Fifth lacks the substance of the other four and has an emotional and formal elusiveness that has not endeared itself either to pianists or to audiences.) The popularity of the Third is reflected by the record catalogues: there are nine available recordings.

Prokofiev got down to serious work on the Third Concerto in 1921, though it comprises themes collected over a period of about ten years or so. He was the most resourceful of composers, rarely throwing away anything that might come in useful later on, so that when he came to write the Third Concerto he had before him a number of bits and pieces. As he tells us in his autobiography: 'As far back as 1911, while working on the First Piano Concerto, I had planned a big virtuoso concerto. I made very little progress with this work, however, and only one passage of parallel triads was preserved. This I now inserted at the end of the first movement of the Third Concerto [bars 219–35].'

Similarly the two themes at the opening of the concerto – the *andante* clarinet melody and the subsequent *allegro* idea – had been conceived some five years earlier. They show two of the principal facets of Prokofiev's style: on the one hand broad lyricism, on the other icy incisiveness, and in the performance by the London Symphony Orchestra with Julius Katchen and Istvan Kertesz these contrasts are sharply made. Few, however, take things at quite such a breathtaking pace as Katchen does and few take it quite as slowly as František Maxian and the Prague Radio Symphony Orchestra on Supraphon. Theirs, to my ears, is a strangely lugubrious performance of such sparkling music; it is the only one of the nine that spills over on to a second side. And, as if that and the thin recording quality were not enough, the coupling is Kabalevsky's unbearably and unrelentingly jolly Third Concerto. It is a record I can well do without.

Not so, though, the one by the New Philharmonia Orchestra under Maazel, with the pianist Israela Margalit. In their performance I am impressed by the tasteful rubato in the wind solos, the beautifully languorous phrasing in the slow introduction (something lacking in the Radio Luxembourg Orchestra's playing for Gabriel Tacchino's performance on the Vox label), and the measured discipline in the quicker music. It is all highly characterful playing and their performance strikes an ideal balance between the grotesque and the lyrical elements of the piece.

For, despite the early critics' comments about it being 'singularly hard and dry as music' the warmer, lyrical moments are many. The London Symphony Orchestra turn these nicely on their recording with Ashkenazy and Previn. Moreover the warm sound of their Decca recording contrasts with the rather harder acoustic given to the performance by Marián Lapsanský on the Royale label; and here, too, things are not helped by a slightly out-of-tune piano. Yet there is much to enjoy in the performance, if not the actual sound; and perhaps one should mention, incidentally, that the position of the piano – or the microphones – must have been changed for the last movement, for the pianist seems suddenly to be playing at the other end of the hall. Again, though, for an interpretation of the first movement I turn to the New Philharmonia and Maazel. The wind solos are all tenderly done here, intertwining quite naturally with the piano's rubato.

The second movement consists of a theme of classical delicacy, and five variations. 'And such variations!', a New York critic commented in 1922. 'Mr Prokofiev poured into them all those amazing tricks of double octaves and rapid chord successions which he plays so easily, and sometimes in the midst of all the tonal bewilderments one suspects that he was on the verge of music. But he always escaped.' Ignoring the latter part of the critic's review, there is indeed much virtuoso piano writing in, for example, the second variation where in Michael Beroff's recording you must be prepared to be blasted by a trumpet. No doubt many would disagree with me, but I dislike recordings that excessively highlight certain instrumental solos by drastically turning up the microphones. Like the close trumpet, there are many other examples in Beroff's recording where an instrument suddenly, and unnaturally, comes to the fore, like being picked up on camera in a televised concert. On record, this sort of thing seems to me to be detrimental to the texture of the piece. This is a pity, because Michel Beroff's performance is electrifying, and I feel sure would have come top of my list had it not been for the uneven recording. The other drawback is that it is available only in boxed set, containing all five concertos and the Overture on Jewish Themes. (I should add that, conversely, Martha Argerich's dashing performance on Deutsche Grammophon has a recorded sound that is often dull and lifeless, often muddy.)

Ashkenazy's performance, which was originally issued in a box, is now, happily, available separately. And what a gloriously radiant performance it is, full of life, and always attentive to the more richly lyrical side of the piece as, for example, in the big tune from the third movement, played first by the orchestra, and then interrupted by the piano skittishly (a fine example of that trait of 'stepping on the throat of his own tune' for which Prokofiev was repeatedly criticised). Yet Prokofiev himself, rather like Rakhmaninov when playing the climaxes of his concertos, does not allow himself to dwell as Ashkenazy does. The composer's superb performance, with the London Symphony Orchestra under Piero Coppola – a recording made in 1932 – is available on EMI's Composers' Interpretation series.

To choose a modern recording of the work is a matter of personal taste. For me there are two recordings which I should like to have: Ashkenazy's with the LSO and Previn at full price; and Israela Margalit's with the New Philharmonia and Maazel at something less than full price though slightly more than medium price. I choose the Ashkenazy simply because of the sheer pleasure it gives to hear him play with such consummate artistry music which he understands so deeply; the NPO record for Miss Margalit's thoroughly idiomatic playing, Maazel's utterly natural pacing of the work, and perhaps above all for the orchestra's warm sound and fine balance, and perfectly phrased instrumental solos, as important in this work as the piano itself.

Recordings Discussed

Prokofiev/London Symphony Orchestra/ Coppola	WR SH 209
Maxian/Prague Radio Orchestra/Klima	Supraphon SUAST 50488
Argerich/Berlin Philharmonic Orchestra/ Abbado	Deutsche Grammophon 139 349
Katchen/London Symphon Orchestra/Kertesz	Decca SXL 6411
*Margalit/New Philharmonia Orchestra/Maazel	Decca PFS 4255
Tacchino/Luxembourg Radio Orchestra/ Froment	VOX STGBY 675
*Ashkenazy/London Symphony Orchestra/ Previn	Decca SXL 6768
Lapsanský/Slovak Philharmonic Orchestra/ Slovak	Royale ROY 2007
Beroff/Leipzig Gewandhaus Orchestra/Masur	HMV SLS 882 (part of 3-record set)

© Geoffrey Norris

Rakhmaninov *Rhapsody on a Theme of Paganini*

GEOFFREY NORRIS

In constant demand as a pianist and conductor, Rakhmaninov found it virtually impossible to concentrate on composition after he left Russia in 1917. In fact of his forty-five opus numbers only six were composed during the last twenty-six years of his life, because the only time he could get down to composition was on those rare occasions when he could spend a lengthy period away from the concert platform. In the early summer of 1934 he had to undergo a small operation, and he was forced to rest for a few months at his villa near Lake Lucerne. It was there that he had thoughts on the piece that at first he called 'Fantasia for piano and orchestra in the form of variations on a theme of Paganini', but whose title was eventually whittled down to 'Rhapsody on a Theme of Paganini'. The rhapsody took him only about six weeks to complete, from early July until the middle of August. And he wrote to a friend in Moscow, 'The piece is rather long, twenty to twenty-five minutes; [and] it's rather difficult. I must begin learning it, but every year I get lazier with practising. I try to get by with some old piece that already lies under the fingers.' However, he did practise it, and performed it for the first time in November 1934 with the Philadelphia Orchestra and Stokowski.

Like his other late works – the Third Symphony, for example; or the Symphonic Dances – the Rhapsody has an incisiveness of rhythm, a pungency of harmony, and a sparsity of texture that many critics at the time contrasted unfavourably with the succulence and sinuous melodic lines of Rakhmaninov's mature Russian works, like the Second Symphony or the Second and Third Concertos. But, more important, the rhapsody was received warmly by audiences, and it provided Rakhmaninov with that new (popular) piece for piano and orchestra that he had been hoping the rather less successful Fourth Concerto of 1926 would be. He included the rhapsody in many of his concerto programmes; he recorded it with Stokowski in the autumn of 1934; and it has maintained a place in the repertory ever since.

There are fourteen recorded versions – or rather thirteen, for one of them crops up twice. So one can afford to be choosy. Valentina Kameniková's performance on Supraphon, with the Brno State Philharmonic under Jiří Pinkas, has to do battle with a huge, cathedral-like acoustic and a thin, nasal recording quality that frankly make for very unpleasant repeated listening. Much the same goes for the version by Marián Lapsanský, with the Slovak Philharmonic under Ladislav Slovak, a new issue on Rediffusion's Royale Label; and there is a similar, undesirable reverberation in the recording made by Philippe Entremont and the Philadelphia Orchestra with Eugene Ormandy (this record suffers too, from some obtrusive surface noise, and also from a wrenching eight-bar cut in the exposition of the theme.)

Julius Katchen's early mono recording – a performance that in itself sparkles with life – has not transferred well to stereo, and the sound is close and woolly. But there is another version by Katchen, his 1960 recording with the London Philharmonic and Sir Adrian Boult with a particularly robust, confident opening, and remarkable clarity in the intricate orchestral detail; for in these late works Rakhmaninov exploited extremely subtly and to the full the individual tone qualities of the instruments.

It has always seemed to me that the Paganini Rhapsody is one of Rakhmaninov's most overtly happy, perhaps the happiest of all his works; and even the use of the *Dies Irae*, which lends such an aura of complete gloom to the work like *The Isle of the Dead,* only casts faint and swiftly dispelled shadows over the rhapsody. The chant occurs first in Variation 7, marked *pesante* but also marked *mezzo forte* and then *cantabile*. You can see what Rakhmaninov meant by such a mixture of terms very clearly in the performance by Ashkenazy, who, in the preceding (sixth) variation, also throws off completely naturally the filigree work in the piano part; and in his almost imperceptible rubato he is followed attentively by the orchestra and conductor.

For more vividly dramatic playing one can turn to Ilana Vered in her fiery performance, again with the London Symphony orchestra, this time under Hans Vonk. But by contrast to the warm and even recording quality of the Ashkenazy disc, this one seems to me at times too cleverly recorded: the piano is nearly always to the fore, but individual microphones seem to be turned up as soon as a particular orchestral section is prominent in the score.

With Variation 10 we come to the end of what we might call the first movement, for the Paganini Rhapsody is not just a string of variations. Rakhmaninov himself likened it to a concerto, and indeed it does fall logically into three sections. Raphael Orozco with the Royal Philharmonic Orchestra conducted by Edo de Waart gives a gloriously impressionistic account of the intermezzo-like Variation 11, and also in the graceful minuet that forms the twelfth. There is a similar delicacy in the performance of Ilana Vered, Katchen, Ashkenazy, and in the 1963 recording by Daniel Wayenberg with the Philharmonia Orchestra and Christoph von Dohnányi. And, if in the performance by Christina Ortiz the twelfth variation does not have quite the same sultry lilt as Orozco brings to it, Miss Ortiz does produce playing of immense power and clarity when, as in some of his concerto slow movements, Rakhmaninov incorporates a Scherzo passage into the middle of these slow variations. You can hear this in Variation 14 where the Paganini theme has been turned upside down, something that has greater significance later on in the piece.

Of course the nub of this rhapsody is the now celebrated eighteenth variation which concludes the slow section. And what an inspired piece of melodic writing it is. In fact it is such a fine melody that it seems unimportant to mention that it is derived from the inversion of the Paganini theme first mooted in Variation 14. Ashkenazy is specially remarkable for the way he leads from the seventeenth variation where, with the gentle rise and fall in the piano playing and the shimmering of the orchestra, he and Previn create a perfect aura of expectation. In Rakhmaninov's own interpretation of the eighteenth variation, he tends characteristically to emphasize the upbeats, which gives it a totally individual, undulating quality; and his playing is affecting in its simplicity and in its absence of self-indulgence. It is a mono recording, with an understandably dull sound, and is available in Volume 5 of RCA's *The Complete Rachmaninoff*. Vásáry, and Daniel Wayenberg, both tend to lean heavily on the eighteenth variation, and for my taste the more enjoyable performances are those that underplay – or at least do not overplay – the music, like, for example, Ashkenazy, Agustin Anievas (who has the added advantage of some rich string playing from the New Philharmonia), Raphael Orozco, and Julius Katchen.

In the final section of the rhapsody the tempo gradually increases with each variation; and the records of Katchen, Ashkenazy, and Orozco are all electrifying in their sheer driving force. In fact their performances are magnificent throughout, with firm orchestral support and a consistency of thought in the interpretations. To choose between them is virtually impossible. Katchen's version, on a medium price label, is a bargain. Orozco gives a somewhat bigger performance than either Katchen or Ashkenazy, but the music is always kept in perspective and there are some sublime effects. But unfortunately his version is available only in a two-record set entitled *A Festival of Russian Music* or in a three-record set including the rhapsody and all four concertos. And so I choose Ashkenazy. His careful grading of tempos and shading of dynamics, coupled with some really fine playing from the LSO, go to make up a performance that is exciting from beginning to end.

Recordings Discussed

Rakhmaninov/Philadelphia Orchestra/Ormandy	RCA AVM3 0296 (part of 3-record set; mono)
Katchen/London Philharmonic Orchestra/ Boult (1954)	Decca ECS 668

Entremont/Philadelphia Orchestra/Ormandy	CBS 61040
Katchen/London Philharmonic Orchestra/ Boult (1960)	Decca SDD 428
Anievas/New Philharmonia Orchestra/Atzmon	HMV ASD 2361
Kameniková/Brno State Philharmonic Orchestra/Pinkas	Supraphon SUAST 50887
Wayenberg/New Philharmonia Orchestra/von Dohnányi	CFP 40267
*Ashkenazy/London Symphony Orchestra/ Previn	Decca SXL 6556
Vered/London Symphony Orchestra/Vonk	Decca PFS 4327
Ortiz/New Philharmonia Orchestra/Koizumi	HMV ASD 3197
Lapsanský/Slovak Philharmonic Orchestra/ Slovak	Royale ROY 2007
Orozco/Royal Philharmonic Orchestra/de Waart	Philips 6747 397 (part of 3-record set)
Vásáry/London Symphony Orchestra/Ahrono-vitch	Deutsche Grammophon 2530 905

© Geoffrey Norris

Rodrigo   *Concierto de Aranjuez*

NOËL GOODWIN

The Concierto de Aranjuez has become the most popular of classical guitar concertos, and Rodrigo himself – who has been blind since the age of three – was 75 in November 1977; he was in London for a brief visit a few days before his birthday. The concerto dates from 1939, and takes its name from the site of the most beautiful of the Spanish royal palaces, in the hills just south of Madrid. Its dedicatee and the soloist at its first performance was Sainz de la Maza, whose record made some years ago is still among those to hand, but its poor quality and rough performance makes it no competitor for the others. It was Julian Bream who first made the concerto widely known in Britain, and his sense of the music's character and locale gives the work a captivating start on his latest disc with the Monteverdi Orchestra conducted by John Eliot Gardiner for RCA. This is Bream's second record of it, which came out in 1975, and although his earlier performance with the Melos Ensemble is still around, it is available now only as part of a three-disc set. Bream's interpretation is almost note for note the same on both, so, as there is no special reason for acquiring the older version if you do not already have it, I am only concerning myself now with the later disc. It is certainly among the best to be had, with a clarity and rhythmic tension that almost implies a sense of drama within the music's character, and contrasts with the softer-grained approach but heavier recording balance of the performance featuring Manuel Cubedo in Pye's Collector series. A curious feature of Cubedo's technique is that, unlike most guitarists today, he uses only the pads of his right hand fingers to strum and pluck the strings, and never the nails. In some of his native Spanish music this could be an advantage, but in this concerto it has a muffled effect in association with the orchestra, and it is overblown by the close focus of the recording balance. So although this is one of the cheaper versions available, it is not one I can recommend.

Another at less than full price is by Siegfried Behrend, who is certainly keen to get things moving. Yet, although the speed at which he takes the opening movement imparts a sense of exhilaration, it seems to me too fast for the music's poetic character. Later in the concerto Behrend's playing becomes merely pale and pedestrian, the support of the Berlin Philharmonic sounding more interesting than the soloist. So that is another performance I feel to be outclassed by its competitors.

John Williams, like Bream, has made a second record of the concerto, while his older one had also become part of a three-disc album. Unlike Bream, though, Williams's interpretation has changed, becoming more relaxed and reflective, and we find expressive orchestral detail and subtle phrasing both from John Williams and the English Chamber Orchestra, conducted by Daniel Barenboim. Williams's earlier record with Ormandy and the Philadelphia Orchestra now seems less rewarding by comparison, and, as I have already mentioned, is only to be had as part of a package album. Apart from Bream, a direct competitor with Williams now is Angel Romero, who sounds more aggressive and forceful in his approach. But, although Romero's playing has a good deal of bite and character, I do not really enjoy the way he tends to snatch at the notes; the orchestral support, too, is rather bland and featureless. This is by the London Symphony Orchestra under André Previn, and later in the movement they seem to be not quite together in phrasing, as well as rhythmically jerky. Romero also has an older (Philips) disc still available, made with the San Antonio Symphony, and I really think this 1968 issue is marginally the better of the two, both in its livelier spirit and balance of detail. It is an appealing performance as a whole, but later in the concerto there is a want of subtlety in much of the detail, and the recording quality lacks depth of perspective. The only other cheaper-price version is a less spirited but still quite buoyant performance with John Zaradin as soloist on Classics for Pleasure. I am afraid I know nothing of John Zaradin, (who is accompanied by the Philomusica of London under Guy Barbier), but as it is put out at about one-third of the recommended price of most of the other available discs, it is obviously worth keeping in mind.

It is, of course, the haunting slow movement which contains the essence of the concerto's charm. This is almost as long as the two outer movements together, with a plaintive lament from the cor anglais at the outset, which is taken over by the guitar and later embellished with runs, turns, and trills, expressing Rodrigo's intention of evoking the grace and elegance of eighteenth-century court life at Aranjuez. John Williams takes this marginally slower than he used to, and the greater freedom of expression and rhythmic flexibility, compared with his older record, helps to sustain the poetic character of the slower pace, dreamier than any other in mood and feeling. A soloist I have not yet referred to is the Venezuelan guitarist, Alirio Diaz, but his strong, flexible technique, and a jaunty spirit he brings to the outer movements, is unfortunately somewhat spoiled by an apparent desire to hurry along the slow movement as well. In doing so he robs the music of much of its poetic feeling and charm. Nor do I find much subtlety or imagination in the solo playing elsewhere in this performance. In this respect I think John Zaradin has more to offer in terms of phrasing and expressive details, and the rest of his performance maintains a very acceptable standard in the cheap-price range. However, the recording balance is inclined to vary in focus, within a more natural perspective for the soloist and orchestra than many of the others, and some of the solo playing verges on reticence, except in the guitar cadenza later in this slow movement.

Julian Bream makes a very arresting first entry in this movement, and its onward momentum is quite different from the dreamy introspection of John Williams. Bream is especially imaginative, and his playing is sharp-featured in the guitar's written-out embellishments to the melodic line. Indeed, throughout this movement Julian Bream remains continually fascinating in his instinctive response to the music, giving it a spontaneity of expression that seems to enrich its character and, for me at any rate, overcomes any passing irritation at the sounds his left-hand fingers make as they slide along the strings. John Williams, as usual, is less obtrusive in this respect, but also a shade more contrived in his slower pace. As I mentioned before, the movement works towards quite a longish cadenza for the solo guitar, which is made to sound almost mysterious by Williams as it builds from a quiet start. Bream is more declamatory, and on the whole I prefer his forthright, almost bitter approach to this movement, which can so easily go soft in the centre. Another detail I admire is the firm spirit and lack of sentimentality when the orchestra's re-entry brings a release of the tension built up during the guitar's cadenza. John Eliot Gardiner and the Monteverdi Orchestra add something of their eponymous composer's vivacity and bright-eyed style to this performance whereas, on the latest record, Previn and the LSO drift almost to a standstill before the cadenza and indulge a syrupy sentiment afterwards. The soloist, Romero, differs from what is written in the score in the first bar and its repeat a phrase later, as well as generating less character with the cadenza. For all its technique as to the manner born, I think Romero's newest record is less rewarding than either Bream or Williams.

The Finale is a dance-type movement based on a simple folk-style theme again introduced by the soloist, who later embroiders it in the style of Spain's sixteenth-century vihuelistas. I find Romero too plodding in temperament and bland in character for the vitality of this movement, and the performance declines into a dull jog-trot. Narciso Yepes, whom I have not mentioned so far, is another soloist with two different performances available. The older of the two (DG), with the Spanish National Orchestra, has more spirited and buoyant playing than Romero, but suffers from a dry, boxed-in acoustic quality, which robs the performance of any bloom. If the sound quality of this record had been richer and wider in its range of colour, I would have given Yepes's performance more consideration, but in overall balance and general character it yields to more recent competitors like Julian Bream, in spite of the marginally slower pace that Bream and his conductor choose for the Finale. Here, I feel, as with his older record, that the slow pace and somewhat sober spirit of his playing in this Finale tells against an otherwise compelling and often exciting performance elsewhere, and the one that I like best of all in the slow movement. The John Williams performance, on the other hand, with its romantic, contemplative approach to the slow movement that drags it out just too much, has a fractionally livelier spirit and more rhythmic bite in the Finale, from orchestra and soloist alike.

If you already possess the older record by either Williams or Bream, I would not suggest rushing to change it. If you are acquiring the Concerto for the first time but do not want to pay the top recommended prices, you might consider the performance by John Zaradin with the Philomusica of London, which is on the Classics for Pleasure label. The best recording quality and most rewarding performances, however, are the newer records by Williams on the CBS label, and Bream on RCA. Remember that Williams is the more introspective and poetic performance, and a slightly slower one, and Bream the more tense and sharper flavour. If it makes any difference, Bream has the very attractive but quite un-Spanish guitar concerto by Sir Lennox Berkeley on the reverse, and Williams the Latin American flavour of the Concerto by Villa-Lobos. Ultimately the choice is like deciding between milk chocolate and plain chocolate – and that is a matter for your taste rather than mine. My own taste, you may possibly have guessed, is marginally in favour of John Williams.

Recordings Discussed

Yepes/Spanish National Orchestra/Argenta	Decca SPA 233
Diaz/Spanish National Orchestra/Frühbeck	HMV ASD 2363
Romero/San Antonio Symphony Orchestra/Alessandro	Philips SAL 3677
Yepes/Spanish National Orchestra/Alonso	Deutsche Grammophon 139 440
*Zaradin/Philomusica/Barbier	CFP 40012
*Bream/Monteverdi Orchestra/Gardiner	RCA ARL1 1181
*Williams/English Chamber Orchestra/Barenboim	CBS 76369
Cubedo/Barcelona Symphony Orchestra/Ferrer	Pye GSGC 15030
Romero/London Symphony Orchestra/Previn	HMV ASD 3415
Bream/Melos Ensemble/Davis	RCA ARL3 0997A (part of 3-record set)
Sainz de la Maza/Manuel de Falla Orchestra/Halffter	RCA CCV 5004
Williams/Philadelphia Orchestra/Ormandy	CBS 77334 (part of 3-record set)

© Noël Goodwin

Saint-Saëns   *Cello Concerto No. 1*

EDWARD GREENFIELD

What on any count is the most striking thing about the first of Saint-Saëns's two cello concertos is the very opening, more urgently exciting than that of any rival work I can think of. From this alone you would think that the concerto was going to be on an epic scale. That is very much the impression given by the young Austrian cellist, Heinrich Schiff, at the start of the concerto, with Sir Charles Mackerras conducting the New Philharmonia Orchestra. The recording quality is outstandingly good, well-balanced in a way that most other versions fail to achieve, with the orchestra on the one hand given full weight and the soloist on the other able to articulate those rushing triplets very cleanly. Schiff and Mackerras seem to keep it in mind too that Saint-Saëns's marking for this opening is not epic-sounding at all but a cautious Allegro non troppo (maybe a sign of his character there).

At something of an extreme, Paul Tortelier on one of the three HMV versions throws caution to the winds, ignores the 'non troppo' and goes at the music very fast indeed. The sad thing is that the recording hardly lets you hear whether his articulation is good or not. The triplets tend to get fused into a sort of rushing cloud of sound. The passion is splendid but after Schiff I do want to hear more of the notes, and Tortelier's speed sounds to my ear rather too breathless. It is not just a question of the soloist's triplets being clouded. I think the recording balance is partly to blame. Perhaps the HMV engineers had second thoughts, for in their next recording of the concerto (with Rostropovich), they then went to the opposite extreme and had the listener practically inside the cello with the orchestra mumbling rather dimly behind. I firmly believe with an instrument as difficult to balance against an orchestra as the cello that some amplification is desirable, but this is far too much. More is the pity when the soloist is Rostropovich, achieving comparable passion to Tortelier, with extra beauty of detail, and the distant-sounding orchestra is the London Philharmonic under Carlo-Maria Giulini. The coupling in this version is the most generous of any, the Dvořák Cello Concerto, but I fear that the unnaturally forward balance of the cello is seriously against a recommendation, and the performance for all its beauties is less spontaneous-sounding than Rostropovich's earlier version recorded in Russia with a balance just as grotesquely weighted in favour of the soloist as the HMV. That comes on the Saga label at bargain price.

The version by Jacqueline du Pré with the New Philharmonia Orchestra conducted by her husband, Daniel Barenboim, is again on the HMV label. And, though the recording was made before both the Tortelier and Rostropovich versions, each poorly balanced in different directions, this time the balance of the cello comes near the ideal. It is also striking, if one compares her with Rostropovich, who tends to get faster as he goes along, to find Jacqueline du Pré commanding the tempo more positively with a steadier view of the main theme but one which is still passionately urgent, and also moulding the transitions with remarkable subtlety of phrasing and shading of the tone. I find Jacqueline du Pré's easing of mood most persuasive and very spontaneous-sounding. To return to Rostropovich in his Saga version, his cello is placed very close, and though his concentration is most compelling his marked slowing for the reprise of the second subject theme is architecturally weaker than, for example, Jacqueline du Pré's treatment, and even as a bargain I would not really recomnend it.

Now for some detail. In the transition into the second section of this one-movement structure, an elegant minuet marked Allegretto con moto, Rostropovich in his more recent HMV version takes a ripely expressive view, but his first unaccompanied entry after the tutti for muted strings is hardly *dolce assai*, very gentle, the marking in the score: it is more a beefy *mezzo forte*. In the Deutsche Grammophon version with Heinrich Schiff and the New Philharmonia Orchestra under Mackerras, Schiff's entry is much nearer *dolce assai*, and the orchestral playing as well as being better balanced is also crisper. At a marginally faster tempo for the Allegretto con moto there is a suspicion of the soloist dragging behind the minuet rhythm, as though the conductor is pulling him along rather than following him; finely controlled but not always perfectly coordinated between soloist and orchestra. That quality of coordination and understanding is precisely what makes Jacqueline du Pré's version with Daniel Barenboim and the same orchestra so remarkable. In this minuet section one comes upon the most controversial point of their reading, the tempo they choose for the Allegretto con moto. It is markedly slower than that of any of the other four versions currently available, and some would no doubt argue that it is too slow, but the rhythmic pointing makes all the difference, so that the slower tempo proves even more charming and persuasive. And Jacqueline du Pré's *dolce assai* in her unaccompanied entry achieves a hushed intensity unmatched by the others.

The extra tonal contrasts in Jacqueline du Pré's performance give it a magic beyond that of the other versions available, even that of a cellist who I usually find is a magic man too, Paul Tortelier. Quite apart from the oddities of balance I mentioned earlier, with the cello sound rather washy and unclean, Tortelier is well below his finest form in the often difficult passage-work. He moulds sections together very persuasively, helped by a fellow-Frenchman as conductor, Louis Frémaux with the City of Birmingham Symphony Orchestra, but there are several technical flaws which for me would be uncomfortable on repetition, such as the suspect octave passage before the lyrical theme emerges at letter O in the score and later the rising scale of high harmonics, always difficult to control. With Jacqueline du Pré at this point it is no longer a tight-rope walk but an upward quest, leading on to far sharper semiquaver passage-work and richly expressive phrasing in the syncopated theme, just as persuasive as Tortelier but more consistently beautiful.

In most respects, in fact, Jacqueline du Pré's performance seems to me in a class of its own, even compared with those of Tortelier and Rostropovich, who in different ways both display comparably creative artistry but who are both let down by their recordings and who interpretatively are not so consistent. Heinrich Schiff is certainly consistent. With his beautifully clean recorded quality and crisp accompaniment from Mackerras and the New Philharmonia, he is the one I would suggest if you strongly object to Jacqueline du Pré's slow tempo for the minuet. He is generally less individual and imaginative, and in the bravura semiquavers of the recapitulation he does not have the same bite, but with flowing tempos in the more lyrical passages the performance holds together well. Yet good as Schiff is as an alternative, I have only one choice when it comes to making a firm recommendation. With Jacqueline du Pré's illness robbing us of her in mid-career her record is all the more to be treasured, an interpretation beautifully matched by her husband Daniel Barenboim with the New Philharmonia Orchestra. In addition there is an equally magical and individual reading of the Schumann Concerto on the reverse to make the perfect coupling. A performance such as du Pré's gives the whole of this compact concerto a sense of scale that matches the epic quality of the opening.

Recordings Discussed

*du Pré/New Philharmonia Orchestra/Barenboim	HMV ASD 2498
Rostropovich/Moscow Radio Orchestra/Stolyarov	Saga 5305
Tortelier/City of Birmingham Symphony Orchestra/Frémaux	HMV ASD 3058
*Schiff/New Philharmonia Orchestra/Mackerras	Deutsche Grammophon 2530 793
Rostropovich/London Philharmonic Orchestra/Giulini	HMV ASD 3452

© Edward Greenfield

Tchaikovsky   *Violin Concerto*

ANDREW KEENER

If the vitriolic critic Eduard Hanslick were alive today, I think he would be startled, to say the least, by the sheer quantity of available recordings: twenty often widely differing views of a composition which prompted his now legendary comment that here was 'music that stinks in the ear' – a hostile reaction indeed, even for Hanslick who had previously been sympathetic towards Tchaikovsky. I think he would be even more taken aback, however, by the sheer variety of approach to the concerto. It is quite rare to find a performance which adheres almost exactly to the notes in the score, and I think it is an interesting point that those which do tend to come from the younger generation of players and that two of these have grown up in a musical tradition very different from our own. Coming as they have, comparatively fresh to the concerto, it is almost as if these players feel no need to embellish a solo part that already offers a fairly wide scope both technically and musically.

Then, if we go right back to those violinists whose careers began in the first decade of so of this century, we come across a school of playing which thought little of adding even more notes to a florid solo passage so that they could show off their highly developed technique. Heifetz offers some very Paganini-like decoration indeed. He is accompanied by Fritz Reiner and the Chicago Symphony Orchestra in a double album from RCA. This also includes the Mendelssohn and Brahms concertos, and there is no denying the tremendous strength and intensity of Heifetz's playing; I just find myself wishing that he would relax a little more: everything seems to emerge at top voltage, and the end result, to my ears at least, is rather exhausting. Those extraneous noises that are all part of the Heifetz personality – brushed open strings, the sound of resined hair on gut, and the like – all tend to add to this fraught impression. Still, Heifetz-followers will know what to expect if they haven't heard this performance already, and it is impossible to ignore the debt that violin technique owes him.

For one reason or another I have also put aside several other versions, many of them reluctantly. With Campoli and Ferras on Decca and Deutsche Grammophon respectively, there is the drawback of having to turn the record over between slow movement and Finale, destroying an essential transition in the process. This also applies to Szeryng's now rather rough-sounding earlier version on RCA 'Camden' – a pity, since there is much to admire, and his remake for Philips strikes me as a little lacking in warmth. Erratic microphone balance spoils Ricci's later recording on Decca's 'Phase Four' label, with some woodwind solos in the Finale sharing the front of the platform with the soloist. Touches that seem spontaneous in his earlier version with Sargent now come over as mannered, and like the recording, rather larger than life. I must also pass over Aron Rosand's sensitive account on Turnabout because of some shaky orchestral ensemble and a few solo passages which would have benefited from a retake or two. This is all very ruthless I know, but there *are* twenty versions to be had, some of them very impressive indeed. Finally, there is Mischa Elman's recording, now available in electronic stereo on Decca's 'Eclipse' label. To hear him play things like the second subject in the first movement is rather like stepping back into an age of more leisurely values, and his equally leisurely vibrato calls for some adjustment from modern ears. Even so the performance has a civilized air about it and at least the recording is good enough to allow this to come through.

Like his First Piano Concerto of some four years earlier, Tchaikovsky's Violin Concerto begins with material that, once heard, makes no further appearance throughout the work. The initial marking is Allegro moderato, and this is not contradicted until two or three bars before the soloist enters. If there is too much of an accelerando as soon as the music gets louder, an already short tutti loses much of its grandeur, and I think that this is what happens with Sir Malcolm Sargent and the London Symphony Orchestra on Ruggiero Ricci's earlier recording on Ace of Diamonds, which still sounds remarkably fresh. The opening melody for the violins is played in a strangely phrased-over manner which tends to rob it of forward movement. The following tutti then has to go at a faster tempo, with the result that it is all over very quickly indeed, and Ricci's first entry is as good an example as any of his rather intense, highly-strung style.

Set beside this kind of approach Mayumi Fujikawa's account with Edo de Waart and the Rotterdam Philharmonic Orchestra on Festivo (Philips) may initially seem a little understated, but it is soon clear that this young Japanese player commands a wider range of dynamic and tone than that of the American player, and the music seems to breathe more naturally at the first solo entry. I also like the way that de Waart points the entry of the cello and bass pedal point: it gives a nice 'lift' to the rhythm without the slightest increase in tempo, and the whole introduction has real weight. Fujikawa is one of the few players to take practically no liberties with the printed notes, and, as I mentioned earlier, she is joined in this respect by Kyung-Wha Chung, Pinchas Zukerman, and Boris Belkin; Arthur Grumiaux in his Philips recording also adds very little in the way of embellishment.

David Oistrakh's performance is the only one featuring a Russian orchestra. As you would expect, there are some bold sounds and grand gestures of the kind familiar from many other Melodiya orchestral discs, but I am not sure that these stem entirely from the Russian style of playing. A cough or two might already have given the game away that this is a concert performance (Moscow, 1968), but it is the only current representation we have of Oistrakh in this concerto. It is exciting to hear this great artist on the spur of the moment, and the tiny flaws that would no doubt have been done again in the studio hardly bother me: what *is* occasionally distracting are the unmistakeable signs that Oistrakh is playing to a tangible audience (sometimes all too tangible), rather than to a future, hypothetical one. The result, while often compelling, is sometimes like watching a film of a live operatic performance where the singers are projecting the music across a distance rather at odds with such closely placed cameras. Even so, there is a fine sense of occasion, and it would make a very exciting second version for your collection.

The first-movement coda of this concerto brings one of those problems which tend to affect Russian Romantic composers in general and Tchaikovsky in particular: that of providing a coda that grows out of the structure of the movement rather than being attached (none too securely) to the end. Rather like the equivalent point in the Fourth Symphony, this coda is a particularly awkward specimen, and when it is approached with such a gigantic slowing up as we find in Milstein's performance with Abbado, the new listener could surely be forgiven for expecting yet another tutti statement of the main theme. Salvatore Accardo and Colin Davis on Philips are more convincing simply by observing the score where there is no indication calling for any holding back; inexplicably it seems to have become one of those 'traditions' to do so, and the transition is much more convincing when, as with Accardo and Davis, it is taken 'in one breath', as it were. I suspect there was a fair amount of detailed preparation for this recording, along with much sympathy between soloist and conductor, and it does show. There is controlled, clean playing from Accardo and, as a recording, this is among the finest available. Accardo is also one of the three players to restore the cuts usually made in the finale.

The central movement, labelled 'Canzonetta', is all too often robbed of its simplicity by over-affectionate lingering and generally too slow a tempo. If you obey the metronome marking, then the gentle lilt of three crotchets to the bar will emerge with no trouble. Any slower and things become bogged down at a very early stage indeed, as they do with Antal Dorati and the London Symphony Orchestra on CBS; indeed, they almost come to a halt for Pinchas Zukerman's first entry, and the fact that things gain some equilibrium at this point says much for Zukerman's ability to lead the ear on at such a measured pace. Vladimir Ashkenazy's way with this introduction is both simpler and closer to the metronome marking, so that when Boris Belkin enters he is allowed to do so with exactly the same sense of movement that the swifter tempo has brought; also, when the music reaches the major, he hardly needs to speed up at all, any fluctuations there are stem more from a subtle rubato than from anything else, whereas many players disturb the mood by a tendency to hurry.

When the very first theme of the movement returns, it appears discreetly on muted strings, and it is important not only to hear it, but to feel that we have somehow come back to base. In Kyung-Wha Chung's recording with André Previn it is expressively played by the London Symphony Orchestra, and beautifully accompanied by the soloist, although not until the solo melody returns a few bars later is there any feeling of recaptulation. In the earlier of Isaac Stern's two available recordings, however, there is something special. With the sound of the Philadelphia Orchestra's strings under Eugene Ormandy, one has a real sense that *this* is the point at which the movement has come full circle rather than with the soloist's melody a little further on. Also, Stern's is the most successful solution I have heard to the problem of rubato in the solo violin theme itself. Very often the conductor has to hold things up while the soloist rounds off the trill with a rather awkward turn. Isaac Stern starts the trill on the upper note, making the printed turn unnecessary, and the music flows on naturally with no problems of coordination between violin, woodwind figures, and pizzicato strings. This performance on CBS Classics has tremendous warmth and brilliance with some of the most positive orchestral support of all. And there's the rub, for there is never any really quiet playing; or at least when you suspect that everyone is playing *pianissimo*, the engineers have brought it up to a healthy *mezzo piano*. If you are an admirer of Stern, though, this record does show him at his best, a rather pointless orchestral cut in the first movement notwithstanding. He is shown to less advantage in his new version, also on CBS, where the orchestral recording tends to be a little hard with some odd shifts of perspective, and Stern sounds very close to the microphone indeed.

When one comes to the transition between slow movement and Finale, William Steinberg and the Pittsburgh Symphony Orchestra (HMV Concert Classics) produce some appropriately rich string-playing set within a helpfully resonant accoustic; instead of gradually relaxing the tempo, however, Steinberg nudges it forward, and he loses a little of the sense of expectancy. There is some splendidly gutty attack from Milstein, and like Stern's pair of recordings, this earlier one does seem to be the more spontaneous of the two. Edo de Waart and the Rotterdam Philharmonic Orchestra are in less of a hurry over this transition and I particularly like the expressive muted strings as the movement slowly ebbs away. Mayumi Fujikawa's entry is suitably passionate without ever overdoing the gypsy element, and the conductor's accompaniment sees to it that we hear the double-bass line. As a result, the rhythm is attractively pointed, especially when the basses are the only instruments playing off the beat – first-rate proof that speed does not necessarily mean excitement. That is not to deny, however, that a top-speed account of this Finale can be exciting as well, provided that it is rhythmically on its toes. Boris Belkin, like Accardo and Grumiaux, gives the concerto absolutely complete. Not that cuts in the Finale affect the issue all that much, since they are only concerned with a few immediate repetitions of this or that phrase. Yet I rather like the way Belkin characterizes the middle scale of the three at the spot where we are accustomed to hearing only one; after all, it is slightly different from the other two and he obviously enjoys pointing this out.

If you do feel Belkin's approach is too high-powered, you may prefer Mayumi Fujikawa's less demonstrative account in the mid-price 'Festivo' series from Philips. It contains some of the most intelligent playing of all, and I find that its refusal to become overwrought brings as many rewards, though of a slightly different kind, as any more overtly emotional approach. The orchestral playing under Edo de Waart is very distinguished indeed, showing the Rotterdam orchestra to be the equal of just about all the competition. At roughly the same price level is Oistrakh's concert performance with Rozhdestvensky and the Moscow Philharmonic Orchestra on HMV 'Concert Classics', a special case, as suggested earlier, but an excellent second version. Of all the more extrovert performances, however, I find the one by Boris Belkin the most rewarding. Even after repeated hearings the excitement never palls, and I put this down to the fact that, however accomplished his technique, Belkin always has time to phrase, to characterize, and to display an attractive sense of humour. With the New Philharmonia Orchestra there is some incredibly accurate playing at a quite fantastic pace.

Recordings Discussed

Elman/London Philharmonic Orchestra/Boult	Decca ECS 569
Heifetz/Chicago Symphony Orchestra/Reiner	RCA DPS 2002 (2-record set)
Campoli/London Symphony Orchestra/Argenta	Decca SPA 183
*Milstein/Pittsburgh Symphony Orchestra/Steinberg	HMV SXLP 30225
Stern/Philadelphia Orchestra/Ormandy	CBS 61029
Ricci/London Symphony Orchestra/Sargent	Decca SDD 126
Szeryng/Boston Symphony Orchestra/Munch	RCA CCV 5015
Ferras/Berlin Philharmonic Orchestra/Karajan	Deutsche Grammophon 139 028
Zukerman/London Symphony Orchestra/Dorati	CBS 72768
Chung/London Symphony Orchestra/Previn	Decca SXL 6493
Milstein/Vienna Philharmonic Orchestra/Abbado	Deutsche Grammophon 2530 359
*Fujikawa/Rotterdam Philharmonic Orchestra/de Waart	Philips 6570 028
Ricci/Netherlands Radio Orchestra/Fournet	Decca PFS 4345
Rosand/Luxembourg Radio Orchestra/Froment	Turnabout TV 34553S
Grumiaux/New Philharmonia Orchestra/Krenz	Philips 9500 086

Accardo/BBC Symphony Orchestra/Davis	Philips 9500 146
*Belkin/New Philharmonia Orchestra/ Ashkenazy	Decca SXL 6854
Szeryng/Concertgebouw Orchestra/Haitink	Philips 9500 321
*Oistrakh/Moscow Philharmonic Orchestra/ Rozhdestvensky	HMV SXLP 30220
Stern/Philadelphia Orchestra/Ormandy	CBS 61029

© Andrew Keener

Telemann   *Viola Concerto in G*

LIONEL SALTER

The viola's original role in the early seventeenth century had been a humble one, as an orchestral inner part reinforcing the bass an octave higher, or, as a special treat no doubt, sometimes doubling the second violins; but its distinctive tone quality was not slow to attract composers' attention, and by the last twenty years of that century it was often being used as an obbligato instrument in baroque opera, especially for laments and arias by lovesick heroes. However, so far as anyone has been able to discover, the first actual concerto to be written for it was very possibly this G major work by Telemann, which he produced (like most of his 170 other concertos) for the weekly concerts he directed in Frankfurt between 1712 and 1721. It is an engaging and typically ebullient work, which includes a beautiful Andante with some unusual expressive harmonic progressions; and it is cast not in the three-movement form of his contemporary Vivaldi, but in the older four-movement *sonata da chiesa* mould – slow-fast-slow-fast – with accompaniment only of strings and continuo harpsichord.

You might think, seeing that this concerto is a lightweight baroque piece, that there would not in fact be much difference of approach between the current recorded versions, particularly since all six quite rightly use a small chamber orchestra. Well, you would be surprised. A very elegant performance, with a persuasive, gentle rhythmic flow, comes from Paul Doktor, whose viola sound is particularly beautiful. He is soloist with the Concerto Amsterdam conducted by Frans Brüggen. Neville Marriner's Academy of St Martin-in-the-Fields, with Stephen Shingles as soloist, takes a fairly similar view of the first movement, though with slightly more romantic ups and downs of tonal nuance in the strings. Moreover, the recorded sound is very fresh compared with the coarse-toned, heavy-handed treatment from Jörg Faerber and the Württemburg Chamber Orchestra, with the soloist Ernst Wallfisch digging into his viola with a kind of truculence that almost suggests he had just had a flaming row. Though the recording is made at a high level, there is a soggy quality of orchestral sound which is very noticeable in the fast movements: the orchestra is too distant and the soloist too near, so that his tone often becomes edgy, though I applaud his admirably true intonation; but frankly I think we can eliminate that one straight away.

There is a disappointingly harsh orchestral sound too in the most recent
version, played by the English Chamber Orchestra, which accords ill with
the silky tone of the soloist, Pinchas Zukerman, He directs the players
himself, and to be honest I think this is responsible for some slight unsteadi-
ness of pace at quite a few points, and for some rather dogged orchestral
playing, as in the bustling second movement. There is a more agreeable
sound, and an altogether lighter, springier feeling – not simply that it is
taken a bit faster – in the version by Stephen Shingles and the Academy of
St Martin-in-the-Fields, though the harpsichord continuo is less audible and
less clean-cut than in the Zukerman performance.

The Andante is the emotional highpoint of this concerto. Before this
Telemann has so far ensured that his solo viola stands out without difficulty:
in the first movement by restricting the strings to quiet chords at the
beginnings and ends of bars, in the second by accompanying the viola most
of the time only with the continuo. Now he alternates the tutti with the
viola supported either by continuo only or by a single line played by the
upper strings in unison. By far the least successful performance here is that
by Lubomir Maly and the Prague Chamber Orchestra, who take it *adagio*
instead of *andante*, thus making it depressingly stolid and robbing it of
rhythmic life. But as they were conspicuously unable to produce any
forward impulse in the first movement either, and their Finale lacks sparkle,
I fear it must be the conductor's fault. There is another point here: a
concerto lasting only thirteen or fourteen minutes is obviously going to
have other works coupled with it, and without going into a tangle of details,
most of the discs we are looking at include either further works by
Telemann or other viola concertos. The Prague Chamber Orchestra
unhappily fills its disc with two entirely bogus concertos purporting to be by
Handel and Johann Christian Bach but actually written early this century
by Henri Casadesus.

It is clear that the Prague players are unaware of this, and along with the
general absence of feeling for baroque style in their performance I am afraid
this rules them out of the running.

When I mentioned the Zukerman recording, I drew attention to the
rather wooden and laboured playing of the orchestra: this lack of sensitivity
is very noticeable in the tuttis of this Andante, which are simply not
phrased at all; and when accompanying the soloist the strings just plod from
one note to the next. The Concerto Amsterdam takes the movement more
lightly: in fact, Frans Brüggen is apparently so determined not to let the
music become romanticized that he allows it a very relaxed rein and makes
it sound almost casual and uncaring – and this despite Telemann's poignant
harmonies.

But, at one point, astonishingly in so stylish an ensemble (the harpsichordist, by the way, is Gustav Leonhardt), instead of just a decorated
cadential figure, Paul Doktor launches out in an extended improvisation
which completely upsets the proportions of the movement (it is nearly a

third as long as the Andante as a whole) and, even worse, ruins the effect of Telemann's magical enharmonic modulation. In complete contrast is the earlier of the two recordings by the Academy of St Martin-in-the-Fields (Oiseau-Lyre). In this the soloist was Simon Streatfield, and I think this version has the right kind of warmth and affection without stepping outside the style.

The last movement is a high-spirited Bourrée which derives much of its rhythmic kick from its driving syncopations. I am rather put off the Concerto Amsterdam performance by the viola's tendency to hurry each time he gets to a passage of quavers and by the odd way Brüggen disturbs the pulse by waiting too long each time at the double-bar; moreover, the very end of the movement is rather untidy. So, having already whittled the field down to two, we have to make a choice between the 1965 and 1976 versions by the Academy of St Martin's. The latter, good as it is, seems to me a fraction cautious, rather as if Neville Marriner had just said, 'Now let's keep it *absolutely* steady and make sure it doesn't run.' Well, it doesn't, but on the other hand it lacks the sheer carefree buoyancy and vitality of the earlier recording, which I find quite irresistible. There is another reason to prefer this earlier St Martin's version (in which, incidentally, John Churchill's continuo is another pleasure), and that is that the more recent issue, in order to accommodate the other works on the disc, is obliged to divide this work with the first two movements on Side 1 and the remainder on the reverse; and really, for a short concerto like this, that does break the flow quite unacceptably.

So to recapitulate: a straight 'No' to the Prague and Württemberg versions; the CBS recording with Zukerman is disappointing in its sound quality, lack of orchestral subtlety, and somewhat uneasy ensemble; the Concerto Amsterdam on Telefunken has the advantage of beautiful playing by Paul Doktor and generally good style, but is marred by some imprecision in the Finale and far too long a cadenza in the Andante; there is the unfortunate break for the turnover, and a few minor reservations about the playing, to take into account in the version by Stephen Shingles and the Academy on Argo; and there is the splendidly spirited Oiseau-Lyre performance by Simon Streatfield and the Academy, in which I could have done without the crescendos applied to the strings' repeated semiquavers in the second movement, but which otherwise wins my vote. The coupling is a miscellaneous programme of Vivaldi, Handel, and Gabrieli, and comes at medium price only.

Recordings Discussed

*Streatfield/Academy of St Martin-in-the-Fields/Marriner (1965)   Oiseau-Lyre SOL 276

Wallfisch/Württemberg Chamber Orchestra/ Faerber	Turnabout TV 34288
Doktor/Concerto Amsterdam/Brüggen	Telefunken AS6 41105
Maly/Prague Chamber Orchestra/Hlavacek	Supraphon 1101057
Shingles/Academy of St Martin-in-the-Fields/ Marriner (1976)	Argo ZRG 836
Zukerman/English Chamber Orchestra	CBS 76490

© Lionel Salter

Beethoven   *Missa Solemnis*

TREVOR HARVEY

With twelve versions of a work as large, in every way, as the Missa
Solemnis my difficulty was to decide how to deal with such an assignment,
especially when most versions are so good. There are only three that I felt I
could overlook with a clear conscience. One, though, I must at least
mention. This is conducted by Gönnenwein for Harmonia Mundi and is
advertised as 'the first recording with original instruments', so it has that
particular interest. Unfortunately the recording is so muddy and the interpretation so undistinguished that I do not feel justified in considering it
further. After all, original instruments maybe, but it still has to stand up to
comparison with the greatest conductors available on record. For the rest, if
you have any one of them, you will have a worthy performance in your
library. But I confess that in order to make some sort of distinction between
them, some of my criticism will sound rather niggling.

But first, what does one expect of performances of this work? It is not
always realized what a revolutionary setting of the mass this is. (And for
that matter, also the earlier and smaller Mass in C.) Think what Beethoven
heard when he was in Vienna: masses by Haydn, Mozart, and lesser
composers, all with solos of the most florid style, as was the custom of the
time. There is no extended solo in either of Beethoven's settings. The
soloists sing as a quartet, usually with the chorus, so the first thing you
want is a balanced solo quartet; the second, a chorus that has immense
vitality as well as the discipline to drop suddenly to hushed singing without
losing the words. On top of all that you want a conductor who digs beneath
the notes and reveals the depth of feeling, giving an interpretation that is
more than a faithful reproduction of what Beethoven wrote down.

Two conductors have recorded the work twice, Klemperer and Karajan.
The very early Klemperer I advise you not to consider. Recordings of this
work need two discs. This has been compressed into one, with consequent
detriment to the sound; and it has also been electronically reprocessed to
give a stereo effect, to its even greater detriment. The two by Karajan are a
very different matter; both made fairly recently and within a few years of
each other: both with the same chorus and orchestra and with Gundula
Janowitz as the soprano in both quartets.

Janowitz is a soprano with a glorious voice but one who takes little care over articulation of words. In spite of Beethoven's emphasis on the meaning of the words (he even had the Latin translated into German, so that he knew the precise meaning), in this instance I do not mind. When she sails into 'Dona nobis pacem'–well, I know the words anyway and her heavenly serenity is quite perfect. She sings on Karajan's HMV recording with the Berlin Philharmonic Orchestra and Vienna Singverein with Agnes Baltsa, Peter Schreier, and José van Dam. There is really very little difference between that and Karajan's Deutsche Grammophon recording, but I do rather prefer the more expansive HMV sound.

Now let us consider an earlier recording. There is no mistaking trumpets of war in the Agnus Dei, very incisively played; nor the dramatic drive of the conductor, Arturo Toscanini, who, in his prime, gave tremendous performances of the Missa Solemnis; and his 1953 mono recording of a Carnegie Hall performance still sounds very well in RCA's latest pressing. His soloists do not match Karajan's but they make a good team – Lois Marshall, Nan Merriman, Eugene Conley, and Jerome Hines – with the Robert Shaw Chorale and the NBC Symphony Orchestra. This is a strong recommendation, especially at its moderate price for the two discs.

As I do commend it to you, I ought, perhaps, to investigate it a little further. Beethoven has trombones in the score but they do not play a note until well into the Gloria, where they make their first entry at the words 'Pater omnipotens' – 'Almighty Father'. This is a dramatic point on which Beethoven seized, and he did not hold back his heaviest brass to this point for nothing, especially as here there occurs the only *fff* in the whole score. All conductors, no doubt, are aware of this but on records they often do not make a great deal of it. Toscanini, however, leaves you in no doubt; and his soloists, if not outstanding, do sing as a balanced team.

If you insist on recent recordings, they come from Sir Georg Solti and Colin Davis. Sir Georg conducts the Chicago Symphony Orchestra and Chorus. The one obvious weakness is in the solo quartet, where the tenor has no real quality; but, if the solo quartet is not quite ideal, the chorus is first-rate in every way, in their hushed singing as well as in their loud, for example in the attack they bring to 'Et resurrexit tertia die' – 'and on the third day He rose again'. Colin Davis, in his performance, shows that a weak tenor can be a grave disadvantage, especially at a tremendous statement like 'et homo factus est' – 'that the Son of God is made man' for he has a splendid tenor in Robert Tear. Davis has, indeed, a very good quartet and I mention the contralto, Patricia Payne, simply because she is not so well known, yet she does some fine things that more famous singers do not, like singing 'Kyrie eleison' in one breath (here even 'Dame Janet Baker fails, yet it is only a phrase of just over four bars).

I might add, before I forget it, that Davis's is a set of three records – as is also the Karajan, to which I have already referred. The third disc contains Beethoven's C major Mass, and you may well think it valuable, as I do, to have for comparison this earlier setting, showing not only Beethoven's complete break with the current Viennese style of mass setting but also the enormous maturity of the later setting we are considering.

Now some short references to other conductors in this highly competitive field. And first of all, Karl Böhm. When his recording first appeared I reviewed it warmly, so I am slightly embarrassed to have to say that now, hearing it again among all its rivals, I think less highly of it. There are two reasons. First, the chorus is from members of the Vienna State Opera; and opera singers are generally not suitable for works of this kind. Its members are would-be soloists – or at least are trained as such, and the choral lines are not as steady as they should be, though everyone sings with unflagging verve and attack. I think Böhm's slow tempos too slow. The very first choral entry, for example, makes both these points – one finds oneself hanging on from one chord to the next; yet Böhm's performance has a great deal to commend it: his solo quartet, for instance, is first-class. So whether you choose it depends on what you think of the chorus and whether you like some very slow tempos.

If you compare the Böhm performance with Jochum's you will find the tempo flows without the music losing any of its grandeur. The Netherlands Radio Chorus is very good indeed, as is, almost needless to say, the Amsterdam Concertgebouw Orchestra, in fact, more than just 'very good'.

One might expect the performance under Giulini also to be among the best. But though it has some splendid singing, it is not as fine as I had hoped. The terribly ragged start of the opening orchestral chord of D major did not of itself put me against it, though it certainly should have been recorded again, and I cannot understand why Giulini passed it. He is most sensitive in slow and quiet music, though for the latter he slows the tempo for the sake of expressiveness, and this I think neither necessary nor in the spirit of Beethoven. Klemperer shows that no relaxing of the exultant *allegro* is necessary and, by the way, the very same chorus, the New Philharmonia, sounds much fresher, and in soft passages its words much more defined, than it does under Giulini.

I am afraid readers of my reviews elsewhere will say, 'Ah, I knew he'd get round to Klemperer in the end.' But hearing so many rival versions in a comparatively short space of time has merely confirmed my view that, to quote Alec Robertson, Klemperer comes nearest to the heart of the matter, to the truth, the grandeur, and spiritual intensity of Beethoven's vision.

Recordings Discussed

Steingruber, Scuerhoff, Majkut, Wiener/ Vienna Symphony Orchestra and Academy Choir/Klemperer	Turnabout TV 37072S

Marshall, Merriman, Conley, Hines/Robert Shaw Chorale/NBC Symphony Orchestra/ Toscanini	RCA AT 200
*Söderström, Hoffgen, Kmentt, Talvela/New Philharmonia Orchestra and Chorus/ Klemperer	HMV SLS 922
Janowitz, Wunderlich, Ludwig, Berry/Vienna Gesellschaft der Musikfreunde/Berlin Philharmonic Orchestra/Karajan	Deutsche Grammophon 2726 048
Giebel, Hoffgen, Haefliger, Ridderbusch/ Netherlands Radio Choir/Concertgebouw Orchestra/Jochum	Philips 6799 001
Janowitz, Baltsa, Schreier, van Damm/Vienna Gesellschaft der Musikfreunde/Berlin Philharmonic Orchestra/Karajan	HMV SLS 979
Price, Ludwig, Ochman, Talvela/Vienna Philharmonic Orchestra and Chorus/Böhm	Deutsche Grammophon 2707 080
Harper, Baker, Tear, Sotin/London Philharharmonic Orchestra and Chorus/Giulini	HMV SLS 989
Popp, Minton, Walker, Howell/Chicago Symphony Orchestra and Chorus/Solti	Decca D87D2
Tomova-Sintow, Eda-Pierre, Payne, Tear/ London Symphony Orchestra and Chorus/ Davis	Philips 6769 001

© Trevor Harvey

Walton   *Belshazzar's Feast*

Walton's text for *Belshazzar's Feast* was chosen for him by Osbert Sitwell
from the old Testament, the Fifth Book of Daniel, Psalms 137 and 81, and
from Revelation, and it tells of the bondage of the Isrealites in Babylon.
Sitwell is said to have modelled the form of the text on the procedure
followed by Charles Jennens, the compiler of Handel's *Messiah*. It is
interesting to recall that Jennens also compiled a *Belshazzar* text for Handel
of somewhat different form from Sitwell's. Even with Sitwell's text, though,
one can imagine a Handelian setting, with recitatives, arias, and choruses;
and the words cry out for powerfully descriptive music, which in Walton's
case has been given mostly to the chorus – even those parts that Handel
would undoubtedly have set as recitative, such as the opening of the work.
This I find sung with characteristic clarity, expressiveness, and firmness
by the male voices of the Philharmonia Chorus conducted by the composer
for HMV. Out of all the six versions of *Belshazzar* currently available, this
is the only opening I can praise unreservedly. The London Symphony
Orchestra Chorus's opening under André Previn (HMV) is one of the best
as regards performance, but their recording suffers from pre- and post-echo
at this point. The Scottish National Orchestra Chorus's performance (RCA)
is also excellent, but the recording is by no means perfect. Both the London
Philharmonic Choir and the Hallé Choir (Decca and Classics for Pleasure)
make actual mistakes, the Hallé's being the most serious. The difficulties
facing a choir in *Belshazzar* are formidable. For one thing, the harmony,
although it is pungently spiced with dissonance, is not so very far away from
what most people regard as normal harmony. If the choir is not very sure of
itself, the discords can easily relax into near-concords, and with this sort of
harmony, a miss is as good as a mile. The choir must also be numerous
enough to maintain the forcefulness of so much of the music and the
extremes of pitch. The syncopated and irregular rhythms must sound as
though they come naturally. The choir carries the bulk of the music, and
although the orchestra is a large one and has an important and colourful
role, the performance stands or falls by the capability of the chorus. I shall
be concentrating on this aspect of the recordings.

    We have three London choirs, and choirs from Scotland and Lancashire –
also an American choir, the Utah Civic Chorale (Vox). I think I must

warn you straight away that in the opening chorus, the American choir sing 'Eye-zay-yah'. (Perhaps this was the received pronunciation when our fore-fathers landed from 'The Mayflower', but it may worry you to hear it sung now.) After that bit of chauvinism, I shall now risk being considered a narrow-minded metropolitan when I say that the London choirs are top of this particular league. They all sing with excellent musicianship and sureness of intonation, and the necessary weight of tone, and it is often difficult to choose between the three. The Scottish National runs this group a close fourth. There are times when they do not sound quite large enough, but they sing very musically and sound refreshingly youthful. The Hallé sound not quite large enough for the demands made upon them and the mistake I have already remarked upon in the opening chorus is not the only one they make. The American choir respond disappointingly to Walton's demands for dynamic contrasts; *Belshazzar* has so much loud music in it that *pianos* and *pianissimos* should be cherished. All these choirs sing with their respective orchestras, naturally.

The Philharmonia Chorus excel particularly in the gentle choruses, such as the second one in the work, 'By the waters of Babylon'. They start with real *pianissimo*, sing sensitively accented chords on the word 'wept', and work up to a moving climax on 'hanged our harps', and they carry the intensity of that languishing phrase right through to the end of the sentence. The bite of the LSO chorus with Previn, too, can be almost terrifying, as indeed the effect should be on the words 'They drank wine again, yea, drank from the sacred vessels', which express the horror felt by the Israelites at the enormity of the sacrilege; and there is a well-paced declamation by John Shirley-Quirk of the words 'Praise ye the gods' and the chorus responds with ferocious energy. Incidentally, Walton is said to have got stuck on the word 'gold' during June 1930, and to have remained stuck, compositionally speaking, until December of the same year.

In the following section, where all the various Babylonian gods, the god of silver, of iron, brass, and so on, are praised, the Scottish National Orchestra chorus come into their own. The phrases in ragtimish rhythm flung between exposed sections of the choir are very nimbly negotiated. (This is the place where the Philharmonia Chorus make their only slips in the work, on their first two entries.) The Scottish National conducted by Alexander Gibson, are specially effective in the section which culminates in march-like ceremonial music. The brass bands, ranged to left and right of the orchestra, stand out well, particularly in stereo.

The baritone soloist has an important role in describing Babylon and then the feast itself, with its turning-point in the narrative, the writing on the wall. In the second of these solos he is largely unacccompanied, in the first completely so. These are key-points in the work, and it is Robert Peterson's singing of the description of Babylon that is one of the main reasons for my not wanting to recommend the Vox Utah recording. He rushes it through, calling irresistibly to mind Walton's own name for it, 'the shopping list', and only just manages to get across the dramatic point of the ending '. . . horses, chariots, slaves . . . and the souls of men'. Peterson also, to my mind, largely misgauges the dramatic effect of the other recitative 'And in that same hour as they feasted came forth fingers of a man's hand'. I am inclined to discount this version, although the choral singing and orchestral playing are adequate if not distinguished.

Of the other baritone soloists, none sings both recitatives correctly in tune all the way through, but Donald Bell in the Philharmonia recording is as close to the written notes as anybody, and his singing does not lack interest and menacing tone, especially in the description of the feast. Perhaps the most authoritative performance is given by John Shirley-Quirk, who seems to have made the part his own, although even he is guilty of occasional uncertainties of pitch in his recording. I was also impressed by Benjamin Luxon, particularly in the description of Babylon, and also in the first appearance of the baritone soloist, with the chorus, in the setting of the words 'If I forget thee, O Jerusalem'. This needs a quality of voice which will be heard against the choir, whilst seeming to lead it. Luxon fulfils both those conditions admirably with the London Philharmonic Choir.

An important task for the conductor in *Belshazzar's Feast* is to establish the various changes of tempo; there are a score of them at least, as well as numerous rallentandos and accelerandos, including what Walton calls graduated *più mossos* – in other words getting faster or slower in the course of perhaps several pages of music. The composer is fairly exact in his tempo directions, although he indicates a certain leeway between the fastest and slowest desirable tempos. There are quite considerable variations in the interpretations of these directions in the different versions of *Belshazzar*. The widest are in the fast passages, and if one takes as an example the rejoicing of the Israelites after the fall of Babylon we find some surprising deviations from Walton's markings. Nobody actually takes this section at the speed Walton specifies, not even Walton himself; in fact he is the slowest, and this has the advantage of allowing all the detail to be very clear, including the trumpets at the words 'blow up the trumpet in the new moon'. Consequently they are able to play their rather exacting semi-quavers beautifully crisply. Solti, with the London Philharmonic Orchestra, is much faster than Walton, and I think it is to the detriment of the detail in the choral singing. The trumpets are not quite able to articulate the quick fanfares distinctly, and Solti drives the music along with rather too much disregard for the difficulties involved; this is particularly evident in some forced jerkiness in the orchestral introduction.

The section beginning 'While the kings of the earth lament', where the chorus sing in a slower, more stately rhythm while the orchestra maintain the previously prevailing faster rhythms, needs breadth of treatment, clarity of line, and beautiful tone, and where the chorus divides into two unaccompanied semi-choruses for 'The trumpeters and pipers are silent', the quality of the individual singers forming the choir, and their ability to blend in small numbers, are important factors. The Philharmonia Chorus give a well-nigh faultless account, bringing a wonderful sweep to the whole section. The balance of orchestra and chorus is just right, the orchestral parts doubling the chorus lines are not obtrusive, and the independent parts in the orchestra are just loud enough to be heard. In the unaccompanied section, 'The trumpeters and pipers are silent', the high, delicately accented chords on the word 'more', of 'shine no more' are especially effective. The London Symphony Orchestra Chorus, who otherwise acquit themselves well in this passage, do not manage these difficult chords as beautifully as the Philharmonia.

Having lamented the passing of Babylon, the Israelites resume their rejoicing, and in this final section, Previn sets off at a spanking tempo well in excess of the composer's directions. For some while after I had bought this recording I continued to be swept off my feet by the sheer exhilaration of Previn's Finale, and preferred it to Walton's, which I have known since 1961 when it was first issued. Now I must confess that I have grown tired of the London Symphony Orchestra version. Previn, as a result of beginning the Finale too quickly, misses the important graduated *più mosso* which leads up to the end of the first alleluias, at which point the choir has a few bars' rest and the composer's direction is *presto*. In an attempt to whip up an even faster tempo here, Previn forces matters so that the alleluias become almost hysterical, especially as the choir is already sounding strained by this time. Walton starts this same section at the fastest limit of his own suggested tempos, a speed which allows him to make that graduated *più mosso*, with the result that the *presto*, with the alleluias flung antiphonally between the two choirs, sounds really effective. The Philharmonia Chorus take the demands made upon them in their stride, and have the stamina to keep up an unflagging intensity right to the end. The wonderful moment when, against the quick triple-time music, the words 'Then sing aloud to God our strength' toll out like a great bell in a very slow four in a bar, succeeds gloriously.

By now it must be clear that my final choice is the Walton version. It is nice to be able to unreservedly recommend a medium-price disc, and there are no problems with the recording quality of this excellent 1977 re-issue. Although I have expressed reservations about the way Previn plays the Finale, you may want to consider his version for its undoubted vitality, the brilliant playing of the London Symphony Orchestra, and for John Shirley-Quirk.

Recordings Discussed

*Bell/Philharmonia Chorus and Orchestra/   HMV SXLP 30236
  Walton

*Shirley-Quirk/London Symphony Orchestra and Chorus/Previn	HMV SAN 324
Rippon/Hallé Orchestra and Chorus/Loughran	CFP 40063
Luxon/London Philharmonic Orchestra and Choir/Solti	Decca SET 618
Milnes/Scottish National Orchestra and Chorus/Gibson	RCA RL 25105
Peterson/Utah Civic Orchestra and Chorale/Abravanel	Vox STGBY 658

© Peter Dodd

Mozart

Serenade for Thirteen Wind Instruments, K361

JOHN WARRACK

It is one measure of the stature of Mozart's Serenade for Thirteen Wind Instruments that it should have been recorded under conductors of the calibre of Furtwängler, Klemperer, Stokowski, and Karl Böhm. No other piece of concerted wind music in the whole history of the genre can match its emotional range, its symphonic proportions, its apparently effortless solution of the problem of how to sustain musical interest throughout a work that lasts the best part of an hour without the contrast and the textural centre of the string ensemble. Mozart himself never repeated the achievement. Many of his serenades and divertimentos are delightful, and enormously enjoyable to play; this serenade, so-called though it really stretches the term to breaking point, this symphony, almost, takes the classical pattern of movements in sonata form, minuet and trio, variations, romance, and so on, and extends this pattern to make a huge structure of seven movements. Obviously Mozart needed more tonal resources for so ambitious a scheme, and the work is scored for two oboes, two clarinets, two horns, and two bassoons (which is normal enough), plus the enriching tone of two tenor clarinets or basset horns, a second pair of French horns in another key from the first pair, and a bass instrument, usually the string double bass, in practice, to give all this wealth of tone a profound and solid foundation.

Jack Brymer's London Wind Soloists' performance of the Serenade is part of a collection of all Mozart's wind music, and his approach is essentially that of a virtuoso wind player leading fellow virtuosos through what is perhaps the greatest piece of large-scale music written for *Harmonie*, or concerted wind. But if this Serenade certainly has its roots in the eighteenth-century serenade and divertimento, it reaches into symphonic territory: already with the very opening one can sense that a conductor such as Karl Böhm, with a long understanding of Mozart's symphonic style, can approach it from a different angle. Karl Böhm's style, with the Berlin Philharmonic Wind Ensemble, is in some ways a richer style than Brymer's, suggesting that what we are embarking upon is more a symphonic experience than a piece of *Harmoniemusik* comparable to other serenades. The opening of Klemperer's performance is still more compelling in this respect, and it is extraordinary that his performance should have been deleted. Another noble performance of symphonic stature is Furtwäangler's; and pitched somewhere between the two approaches is Barenboim's, with members of the English Chamber Orchestra. In many ways he achieves the best of both worlds, in that he allows the performers to retain a feeling of being solo wind players, while suggesting a symphonic scope and control in his handling. His recording, from HMV, is also particularly responsive to the demands of wind instruments: Mozart was writing for a novel combination of sounds, and made full use of it, and so part of the musical point lies in the use of original and fascinating combinations of textures which need a modern recording to do them justice.

Another conductor who takes the work as one needing strong interpretative direction is Willem van Otterloo, who gives a lively performance with the Sydney Symphony Orchestra. He takes the opening faster, and moves into the Allegro with a bright sense of rhythm; this, however, is not so well sustained, for, brightly as he sets off, the rhythm does come to have rather too much the same kind of bounce, so that instead of being constantly fresh it grows a little insistent. Karl Böhm takes a more Romantic, sometimes charmingly lyrical, gentle view of the music – one it can well sustain, and which emerges to the surface of the music later in the work. He has much more of Mozart's subtlety in his approach than van Otterloo.

One performance is of a special nature, and this is the record by the Collegium Aureum. As many collectors know well, this is a group which specializes in the revival of period instruments, or their reconstruction by modern makers, and their uses in well-studied performances. From these players we hear Mozart as he may well have sounded in the ears of his contemporaries, and indeed in his own imagining ear. Without going over all the arguments pro and con the use of period instruments, I would just say that reconstructing the instruments is not the same thing as reconstructing the style of performance, and that their use should be a starting point and not its own justification. Barenboim often takes the music much faster, and you may find it too fast, but he brings it off because he has a sense of the music's brightness and quickness of invention and brilliance of contrast, which is lacking in the more laborious if conscientious performance by the Collegium Aureum.

The second movement would normally be a slow one, but Mozart inserts a Minuet with not one but two Trios, before reaching the most profound of his seven movements, the Adagio. Here he makes the richest use of his textures, with the melody shared between oboe and clarinet over throbbing rhythms in the middle parts and a stalking bass. Jack Brymer and his players keep these texture very open and lucid. His performance in this movement is nicely poised and well balanced, but it does have a slightly perfunctory tinge to it, especially when one turns to Karl Böhm, who plays this Adagio with the intensity of one of Mozart's major slow movements, which indeed it is. He encourages his players to caress the accompaniment figure that runs through the movement, rather than keep it light and precise, and this does help to give the exchanges between oboe and clarinet a melodic warmth somewhat lacking in the Brymer version.

Karl Böhm's players are the Berlin Philharmonic: twenty-five years before his recording was made, Wilhelm Furtwängler made a version in 1947 with the Vienna Philharmonic. The recording cannot match modern stereo techniques, of course, but it has a remarkable depth and range; and Furtwängler's performance is unique. Some of the actual playing lets him down: the intonation is poor in places, and the ensemble suffers from his curious, hesitant stick technique when the precision of wind instruments is involved, whereas with strings and the full orchestra it could mean a warm, almost vocal easing in to the music. The opening of the Adagio does not come off ideally, but by the end Furtwängler's interpretative powers have compelled the players to his vision, and he rounds the music off as if he too believed in this as one of Mozart's great slow movements.

Mozart follows the slow movement with a second Minuet, again giving it the extra weight of two Trios to balance the first Minuet; and then comes another slow movement. But having put so much into the Adagio, he here writes a lighter Romanze, answered in its second half by an Allegretto. Brymer plays the Romance elegantly and with a feeling of its lightness by contrast with the Adagio. Karl Böhm, on the other hand, suggests that this is a more substantial slow movement, and in the second strain, where Brymer has the bassoon octaves played as little more than a rhythmic underpin to the held chords and melodic movement above, Böhm makes them more atmospheric, even foreboding, with a feeling of drama and suspense hanging over the music. There is no right or wrong about either of those two approaches, but Böhm does make a stronger contrast between the foregoing Minuet and the Theme and Variations which follow.

The six variations which succeed the theme might almost have been designed to reflect the varying approaches to the theme which different conductors and groups of players can feel; and not surprisingly the various recordings show contrasted approaches, with different artists at their best in different variations. The clear textures and straightforward music of Variation 1, for instance, particularly suit the style of Jack Brymer's London Wind Soloists. The yearning phrases and Romantic feeling of Variation 4 suit Karl Böhm's symphonic approach better, and he makes of this movement a very affecting little episode, although he is rather less alert and fresh than Brymer in the earlier variations. Then, instead of making the obvious contrast with a lighter variation, Mozart plunges into the most substantial of the whole set, a deeply felt Adagio in which he makes use of the full tonal resources of his ensemble in a manner hardly before suggested even in the very opening of the work and in the second movement. The excellent recording which HMV have given Barenboim is a real musical help here, especially in the second half of the variation, when the clarinets and basset horns set up rich, softly stirring arpeggios as a bed of sound over which the solo oboe can sing its melody.

On the whole, I find Barenboim's performance with the English Chamber Orchestra the most satisfactory all-round performance. Brymer's Soloists are no less expert, certainly, but the atmosphere of playing the work as if it were much the same creative enterprise as Mozart's smaller wind serenades and divertimentos does underestimate the imaginative range of the music. Böhm's performance is a very beautiful one, but it lacks the crispness which Brymer certainly achieves, and some of the episodes are somewhat inert, however beautifully Böhm responds to the emotional seriousness of the work. Van Otterloo is clear, but misses some of the most important opportunities; and another performance which I have not so far mentioned, by Edo de Waart, is also somewhat on the light side, though if you respond to the briskness and the engaging sparkle of his music-making, you may enjoy his performance as part of a boxed set of Mozart's wind music. But if there is to be a single selection, then I feel in no doubt that the most satisfying version is by Barenboim, for its virtuosity, its response to the richness of the scoring, its symphonic understanding, and at the same time its enchanting gaiety and wit.

Recordings Discussed

Vienna Philharmonic Orchestra/Furtwängler	Unicorn WFS 10
Netherlands Wind Ensemble/de Waart	Philips 6747 378 (part of 7-record set)
London Wind Soloists/Brymer	Decca SDDL 405-9 (part of 5-record set)
Berlin Philharmonic Wind Ensemble/Böhm	Deutsche Grammophon 2530136
Sydney Symphony Orchestra/Otterloo	RCA GL 25015
Collegium Aureum	HM 1C 065 99654
*English Chamber Orchestra/Barenboim	HMV ASD 3426

© John Warrack

Schoenberg   *Pierrot Lunaire*

STEPHEN WALSH

Schoenberg would have enjoyed his *Pierrot Lunaire* featuring in a collection of this kind – that is, he would have enjoyed the hint of popularity this implies. The fact that *Pierrot* can currently be had in five different recordings, despite several recent deletions, would perhaps not have surprised him greatly. He firmly believed that his music could be enjoyed by the ordinary listener, even though it upset the 'expert judges', as he contemptuously labelled those who attacked his music in print. Unlike most of Schoenberg's works, *Pierrot Lunaire* was a success from the start: it was enthusiastically received by its first audience in Berlin in 1912, when the actress Albertine Zehme, 'trembling and fearful' as Webern later recalled, stood alone in front of a screen concealing the five instrumentalists and declaimed the twenty-one Giraud poems in that peculiar and difficult technique called *Sprechgesang* or 'Speech-song', which Schoenberg had invented for the occasion. *Pierrot Lunaire* was essentially an entertainment, a cycle of cabaret songs, though written in a supposedly difficult atonal idiom. This is still the best spirit in which to enjoy the work, despite its rather heavy reputation as a sacred text for the avant-garde of our own day.

Although much performed nowadays, *Pierrot* is by no means always that *well* performed. The instrumental parts are difficult enough, but the voice part is of exceptional difficulty, and is still in some respects the subject of controversy. Schoenberg left fairly precise instructions as to how the *Sprechgesang* was to be delivered, but unfortunately his notation is rather imprecise, and for that reason singers often treat the part as a more or less free declamation with only the vaguest reference to the written music. Schoenberg's notation is based mainly on exact written pitches, with a cross through the tail of each note to indicate *Sprechgesang*. The idea of the technique was that the singer should attack the note as written but quit it at once, either rising or falling, as in a kind of stylized or rhetorical speech. But the direction, degree, and speed of departure from the given note were left to the singer's taste. Of course we can guess what kind of effect Schoenberg had in mind, but an exact realization of his written text is still not at all easy; indeed I would go so far as to say that I have never heard one. In assessing the recorded performances, therefore, one had to fall back on the more personal and perhaps more nebulous criterion of what is convincing.

Incidentally, it is a curious fact that among the five singers there is not a single native German-speaker. One of them, the jazz singer Cleo Laine, actually performs the work in English, though this fact is nowhere indicated on the sleeve of the record, which is issued by RCA.

So far as musical style is concerned the performances cover practically the whole range of possible approaches to the work, from the freely declamatory type which practically ignores Schoenberg's written pitches, to the rather straight-faced sung type, done with exquisite tone and based on definite pitches (if not necessarily the written ones). The recently issued performance conducted by Pierre Boulez, with the singer Yvonne Minton, comes into this second category. Listening to a Boulez performance of *Pierrot Lunaire*, by the way, one should remember that, as a composer, Boulez has always been profoundly interested in systematic pitch-structure. His most *Pierrot*-like work, *Le Marteau sans maître*, has an elaborate scheme of graded pitch, and one cannot help wondering if he is not therefore a trifle impatient of Schoenberg's comparative vagueness in this respect. Yvonne Minton is accompanied by a veritable team of all-stars, including Pinchas Zukerman, the American cellist Lynn Harrell, and Daniel Barenboim at the piano. The playing is superb, but the recording does not always show it at its best. There is a somewhat hollow acoustic which occasionally masks detail.

However beautiful we may find Yvonne Minton's singing, we can be practically certain that Schoenberg had something different in mind. There is really not much 'sprech' to her 'gesang'. But a fair criticism from the other side would be that while mostly singing the notes Miss Minton does not always sing the written notes. In other words she seems to interpret *Sprechgesang* to mean singing approximately the notes written in the score. But Schoenberg, whose own pitch sense was highly developed, almost certainly chose the pitches he wrote down for definite reasons. To sing other notes frequently distorts the harmonic image.

The performance by Mary Thomas with the London Sinfonietta under David Atherton may be less beautiful than the Boulez version, but it is also a great deal more alive. Mary Thomas uses exact pitch as a launching-pad for a vigorous interpretation of each song. Schoenberg warned against characterizing each song according to the verbal sense, without reference to the music, but it is a great feature of Miss Thomas's performance that she achieves so much character within the given musical framework. Her experience as soprano in Peter Maxwell Davies's group, the Fires of London, stands her in good stead in *Pierrot Lunaire*. She has developed a *Sprechgesang* style which feels completely natural, and which is therefore a musically flexible instrument. She has in any case a remarkably athletic voice, is an instinctive vocal actress, and at the same time is an exceptionally intelligent musician. Schoenberg makes great demands on all these qualities. In the third song, 'Der Dandy', for example, the music exploits violent dynamic contrasts, and different types of vocal production, including normal singing, and a toneless whisper which Miss Thomas manages to invest with spinechilling venom.

It would be hard to overstate the problems posed by music of this kind. Somehow the jagged expressionist contours have to contribute to the music's impetus. But it is hardly surprising if, just as often, they tend to break it down into a mosaic of individual gestures. Marie-Thérèse Escribano, for instance, in a recording conducted by Friedrich Cerha, is not heard at her best in these more expressionist songs. Her voice is rather light, but extraordinarily attractive, full of expressive subtleties and curious powers of suggestion. For instance, she has the ability to smile with her voice, and to invest individual words and even syllables with a delicate sensuality. But in songs calling for exceptionally dramatic treatment, or dark vocal colouring, she runs into difficulties.

Whatever Marie-Thérèse Escribano's limitations, however, they pale into insignificance beside Cleo Laine's – at any rate so far as Schoenberg is concerned. It is easy to see why a gifted singer of Miss Laine's type might attempt this work: it is, as I said earlier, a cabaret work, an entertainment, and it calls for histrionic gifts that are more likely to come naturally to the popular entertainer than to the classical singer. But it also calls for musical abilities of a particular and specialized variety. The fact that the written pitches are not meant to be sung accurately does not mean, as I have suggested, that they are arbitrary or unimportant. The technique is not easier of course, but even harder, than that needed for Schoenberg's more conventional songs. Cleo Laine makes a valiant effort, nevertheless, and is beautifully accompanied by the Nash Ensemble under Elgar Howarth. Her admirers will find much to enjoy here, even though what she sings often has little to do with Schoenberg and is sung, as I mentioned earlier, in English. Hers is the far extreme in *Sprechgesang* interpretation, a long way from the almost sung performance of Yvonne Minton. Comparing the two extremes, it is tempting to feel that while the sung performance has self-imposed limitations it does also have a musical assurance and precision which Cleo Laine's performance lacks. This comes out particularly in the more exacting songs in the second part of the work, where the tone is generally more violent and the imagery more grotesque and fantastic than in the two outer parts. Here Pierrot becomes obsessed by nightmare visions which threaten to destroy him. For instance, in the so-called passacaglia, 'Nacht', he is haunted by giant moths, whose wings shut out the sunlight and suffocate the heart. The song is one of Schoenberg's most famous contrapuntal inventions, being derived almost entirely from a ten-note row whose first three notes form a series of overlapping folds – a graphic image for the giant moth-wings of the poem, shutting out all musical light. This song shows Yvonne Minton's mezzo register to advantage, particularly on the low-lying phrase to the word 'Verschwiegen', which Schoenberg, with characteristic ruthlessness, directs to be sung.

It is, in fact, worth comparing this with a conventional type of *Sprech-*

gesang performance such as the one by the Hungarian soprano, Erika Sziklay, with the Budapest Chamber Orchestra under Andras Mihaly. Miss Sziklay is at some pains to realize Schoenberg's notation, but she seems not to have got beyond the stage of being limited by the convention, rather than liberated by it. For instance, she takes Schoenberg's instruction about rising or falling from each note rather literally, and the effect is studious rather than artistic, though technically the performance is good, and the accompaniment generally excellent. However, this version, which comes from Hungaraton, raises a further problem in connection with this work: the question of recording quality. Schoenberg's ensemble was a drastic innovation in its day, and even now it cuts across conventional ideas of blend and fusion of tone. The idea must have been to invent a group which would be at the same time expressive, colourful, highly flexible, and versatile, but above all clear. In a recording we need to hear each instrument distinctly and equally yet not with that violent studio clarity which destroys all musical integration. The Hungarian recording is not good in this respect, but nor are some of the others. The CBS Boulez version, as I have already suggested, is not altogether favourable to the instruments, though this may also have something to do with the bel canto character of the performance itself. The best recording, and indeed much of the best playing, is in the Decca version with Mary Thomas and the London Sinfonietta with David Atherton. The balance there is almost ideal. Moreover the recording shows how a true *Sprechgesang* style brings the instruments into particularly sharp focus because their pitch is firm and established. Schoenberg makes a nice point out of this in a song like 'Parodie', where the voice is in canon with the viola and clarinet. Because the vocal pitches are inexact, the canon sounds ironic. Mary Thomas and the London Sinfonietta bring this off brilliantly. They are helped by the well-focused recording, and the playing sets a standard which is hard to match.

Marie-Thérèse Escribano is accompanied by an ad hoc team of German instrumentalists under Cerha, and although the playing is good the ensemble is often rather untidy – in a work where rhythmic outline is of paramount importance. Very surprisingly there are also occasional rhythmic imperfections in the performance by Yvonne Minton and Boulez. These mainly come in the fitting of the voice to the accompaniment. In the exquisite barcarole, for example, which forms the penultimate number in the work, inaccuracies of this kind slightly detract from the beauty of the performance.

For all the good qualities of Yvonne Minton's performance, my own final preference is strongly with the version by Mary Thomas and the London Sinfonietta. This is partly because of the superb quality of the playing and recording. But above all because of the brilliance of Mary Thomas herself, who, alone among the five singers, gives a full-blown performance of the work, with a big histrionic and gestural range, yet backed up by firm musical discipline. I would be the last to pretend that her voice was the equal of Yvonne Minton's, purely as an instrument. In particular she lacks Miss Minton's strength below the stave. In the end *Pierrot Lunaire* is hardly to be defined in terms of vocal beauty. What counts is the ability to turn Schoenberg's detailed, taxing, and sometimes ambiguous instructions to vigorous account in projecting the powerful and volatile atmosphere and frequent wit of the poems. In this Mary Thomas is consistently successful.

Recordings Discussed

Sziklay/Budapest Chamber Orchestra/Mihaly	Hungaraton SLPX 11385
Escribano/Ensemble/Cerha	Turnabout TV 34315S
Laine/Nash Ensemble/Howarth	RCA LRL1 5058
*Thomas/Members of the London Sinfonietta/ Atherton	Decca SDD 520
Minton/Ensemble/Boulez	CBS 76720

© Stephen Walsh

Schubert

Piano Quintet in A, 'The Trout'

STEPHEN DODGSON

Half of the sixteen current recordings of the 'Trout' Quintet have been available for a number of years and still include some of those I enjoy the most. For instance, there is Jörg Demus, now on Deutsche Grammophon's bargain Heliodor label. The string players are the appropriately named Schubert Quartet, very much of one mind with their pianist in his lively sense of motion, and phrasing with a strongly springing emphasis to it. The recording favours the piano just too much, but this has never been more than a marginal reservation to my mind. In other respects the tonal qualities of both piano and strings are remarkably good, and one of the qualities which always stands out in this account of the 'Trout' is the conviction it gives one of that unpremeditated freshness necessary in so much of Schubert's music, and perhaps nowhere more so than in this quintet. Higher up the price-range, Deutsche Grammophon have two other possibilities, but both are surpassed in musical appeal, as in price, by this bargain version on Heliodor.

Demus also appears in a newer version, this time playing a fine Viennese Conrad Graf piano of the period, with string players of the Collegium Aureum playing on gut strings. This too conveys a lively freshness, and the graceful lightness of string tone, especially from the double-bass, is another appealing factor. But, possibly through insufficient belief in the carrying power of the Graf piano, Demus here seems to exaggerate most of his points of emphasis. Also the swimmy excess of reverberation does little to assist the authentic early nineteenth-century tonal transparency presumably aimed at. This performance from Harmonia Mundi is a little disappointing I think; at least my instinct is for Jörg Demus's older and much cheaper version on Heliodor.

Of the newer versions, one of the most winning happens also to be one of the cheapest; a goodish recording from Classics for Pleasure, with principals of the London Symphony Orchestra, and Moura Lympany the pianist. This is marvellously unaffected, and a pleasure to meet Moura Lympany as a chamber music pianist with such a sure instinct for a transparent balance. The little eight-bar piano solo in the first movement (bars 84–92) provides a good example of Moura Lympany's approach. The exceptional clarity and sparkle of the closing section which then follows is most appealing too, with its crisp and telling dynamic contrasts. By a margin, I think this, much newer, bargain version surpasses the one with Demus on Heliodor.

There are three versions of the Trout Quintet available from Philips. The most obvious contender for attention is probably that by the Beaux Arts Trio, with guest artists to make up Schubert's oddly-formed quintet of string trio, double-bass, and piano. It has all the detailed beauty and finesse one has come to expect of this prestigious ensemble, and it is superlatively recorded. Tonally the style is a little on the opulent side, with a constant and considerable rise and fall; not actually quite my taste, which – in this music at least – is for something much less elaborate. But the Beaux Arts are not to be faulted I think, and the easy flow of their Andante tempo in the second movement is beguiling.

The newest 'Trout' of all, also from Philips, features Alfred Brendel and the Cleveland Quartet. Perhaps it was only because my expectations were pitched high that I found this increasingly disappointing the more I listened. The string playing is very distinctly sweet, and leads to rather sluggish tempos both in the second movement and in the variations of the fourth movement. Yet the finale is almost perversely fast. Within movements, too, there tend to be prominent hitches of tempo prompted mainly, it seems, by Brendel constantly stressing the piano part, underlining phrasing that would be just as intelligible and certainly more charming if only he would allow it to be simpler and generally quieter. In addition to Brendel and members of the Cleveland Quartet, Philips have recently re-issued in their mid-priced Festivo series a version of some years ago by Ingrid Haebler and a string ensemble led by Arthur Grumiaux. Here is the opposite view from Brendel's, with Ingrid Haebler lightweight almost to a fault, the tempo a little faster and very evenly held; and I must say I like it for both. Nowhere does Ingrid Haebler show to quite such telling effect as in the second movement, though whenever delicacy and transparency are the desired attributes (which is often in the 'Trout' in all conscience) she is a delight. In the faster movement, she is perhaps a little dull in character; but then, there is some of the best of all string playing in this version, from Arthur Grumiaux himself in particular. So, as far as the possibilities from Philips go, I do not myself have too much difficulty preferring this mid-priced Festivo, though with the Beaux Arts not so far behind.

I should like to consider next a recording that is, with ample reason, probably the best known and best loved version of the 'Trout' there has been since the arrival of the LP record. It is by Clifford Curzon and members of the Vienna Octet, led by Willi Boskovsky, and has long been available in Decca's Ace of Diamonds series. It is in the last two movements where, to my thinking this version is supreme. The opening Allegro Vivace I have always found a fraction too deliberate, as though the *vivace* had been left out. The Scherzo movement, which lies third of the five, has a Trio section so much slower, that, although I have become used to it, I still find upsetting to the unity of the movement as a whole. However, on reaching the variations, all doubts evaporate, with the Trout itself swimming into the picture at the true Andantino it is so seldom permitted. For Curzon and members of the Vienna Octet these variations are essentially different aspects of the same thing, as opposed to the notion of making each variation a miniature movement on its own, deriving from a common source. This latter type of approach is associated with a generally more romantic view of the movement; usually introduced by a theme at slow tempo, each succeeding variation a little faster leading to the more dramatic fourth. As this variation has great aptitude for sinking away to a deep and distant darkness, it immediately suggests a slow nocturne for the fifth variation with its cello solo.

I am not trying to say that the Andantino of the theme must be rigorously applied throughout. Still less am I trying to deny the movement a growing sense of twilit romance into which the song itself finally bursts with a sudden playfulness. One of the best performances of this movement, indeed perhaps of the whole quintet is by the Melos Ensemble (Terence Weil, the cellist) which shows how much more effective the romantic touch can be if hinted at more than too openly indulged. Of all the more romantic views of the quintet, this, by the Melos Ensemble, is the subtlest; it is the only one which never loses sight of the music's freshness and immediacy, and for this it owes a lot to the infectious poise and rhythm of the pianist, Lamar Crowson. Of the full-priced versions, with highest standards of recording, this is my final choice. However, a quick summary of the other versions is necessary as well as a general thought or two about the finale.

As I have mentioned, Curzon and the Vienna Octet are supreme in the last two movements. The finale in their hands is a dance, with a springing rhythm, and not too fast. The recording is now twenty years old, but the internal balance is so good that you hardly notice the lack of dynamic range or its shallow tone. It is a performance which stresses the youthfulness and immediacy of the music, which is certainly the way in which I respond to the 'Trout' most vividly. Naturally then, I am drawn to the bargain version on Classics for Pleasure with Moura Lympany. Here, the Finale is, I think, the least good movement, mainly because it is a fraction too fast. Yet, despite the Finale, I can strongly recommend this recording; and here too I should draw attention to another bargain version, by the Smetana Quartet and Jan Panenka on Supraphon, since on no other record does the Finale dance with quite such an infectious and steady gait. This is a version in which the whole work has a rosy-cheeked, rustic quality, with one perfectly simple drawback. Every tempo throughout the work is moderate, bouncy, and remarkably alike. It is as though the players were all geared up for this finale ages before they got there. However, if, at the very front of your mind, you have a picture of Schubert writing this music as a joyful holiday greeting, then this recording probably conveys that sensation most vividly, even if Panenka is a shade less interesting than his colleagues of the Smetana Quartet. All the same, the performance by the Melos Ensemble, without emphasizing this aspect nearly so much, never forgets it either. It also never misses those frequent moments of poetry, the very unconsciousness of which it is also important to convey.

Recordings Discussed

*Curzon/Members of the Vienna Octet	Decca SDD 185
Demus/Schubert Quartet	Deutsche Grammophon
	2548 122
Kentner/Hungarian String Quartet	Turnabout TV 34140S
Panhoffer/Vienna Octet	Decca ECS 617
*Melos Ensemble	HMV ASD 2328
Eschenbach/Koeckert Quartet	Deutsche Grammophon
	2535 332
*Lympany/Members of the London Symphony Orchestra	CFP 40085
Rhodes/Hortnagel/Beaux Arts Trio	Philips 9500 071
Gilels/Zepperitz/Amadeus Quartet	Deutsche Grammophon
	2530 646
Panenka/Smetana Quartet	Supraphon SUAST 50174
Demus/Collegium Aureum	HM 1C 065 99701
Haebler/Arthur Grumiaux Ensemble	Philips 6570 115
Brendel/Cleveland Quartet	Deutsche Grammophon
	9500 442

Schubert   *String Quintet in C*

JOHN WARRACK

The greatness of Schubert's C major Quintet is not easily encompassed by any one ensemble, ranging as it does far across different kinds of musical experience. The group that can take in its stride the fresh, open-air music that dominates the finale may underestimate the darkness and complexity of the first movement, and for this reason I set aside the Vienna Philharmonic Quartet record. A group of great musicians may respond to the most intense qualities in the music but lack something which comes from long experience as a regular chamber ensemble, and this led me to prefer other versions to the old CBS record, despite the presence in the ensemble of Isaac Stern, Tortelier, and Casals. Others I rejected, for different reasons, were by ensembles based on the Tatrai, Alberni, and Weller Quartets, leaving me five for fuller consideration.

The Lansdowne Quartet, with Amaryllis Fleming as second cello, on World Records offers clear, well-balanced playing, but it seems to underestimate the amount Schubert can manage to say even in a work's opening bars. In harmonic terms, here, it is a C major chord, then a diminished seventh, then a phrase in the minor before a return to C major; or less technically, Schubert sounds the key-chord of the whole work, then poisons its freshness with the Romantic chord of the most sinister associations, which brings a tinge of minor key sadness before the major key chord returns – all in six bars, but six bars which tell us that a complicated emotional experience lies ahead. More than the Lansdowne, the Amadeus Quartet with William Pleeth on Deutsche Grammophon seem to appreciate these implications. They place the harmonic accents carefully, emphasizing that this is the material of Schubert's inspiration. The Aeolian Quartet with Bruno Schrecker on Saga are also appreciative of what is involved, but they play the opening in a manner which makes the music seem still more disturbed, even shocked. It is of course possible to over-emphasize points, and this I think the Juilliard Quartet with Bernard Greenhouse do, on their CBS record. However, they play with great intensity, and they try to bring out the strain and the drama of the passage that immediately follows the opening. It is very much more than the conventional bridge passage leading into the second subject, and here the Juilliard Quartet bring a fervent quality to the music, continuing this well into that sublime second subject.

Another, and I think more perceptive, view of the music is to play the stormy bridge passage as if it were the emotional crisis already threatened in the opening bars, so that the second subject then takes its place as something touching and resigned in the wake of the crisis, needing very calm and serene playing for its point to be made. I find that the Melos Quartet of Stuttgart take this view. They have as their second cellist none other than Rostropovich, on Deutsche Grammophon. This is an effective, strong performance, and one that understands the subtleties in the work without losing sight of its breadth. At the end of this first movement, Schubert compresses all his materials into an extraordinary passage – both his main subjects, the emotionally crucial bridge passage, finally his home C major, still troubled by chromatic notes. It needs playing of great understanding, neither understated as by the Lansdowne nor overstated as by the Juilliard: the Aeolian and the Amadeus are both good with it, but it is the Melos who complete this astonishing movement most fully and satisfyingly.

The Adagio opens with a piece of scoring beautifully showing Schubert's resourcefulness, for in effect it is a string trio of the middle instruments with decorative comments from the first violin and a pizzicato bass from the second cello. The Lansdowne give this a calm, relaxed performance that makes the effect very nicely, and their playing is straightforward and unaffected; but, as always with Schubert, great expressive resources lie within even his most innocent-looking music. The Juilliard Quartet try rather too hard to make a powerful effect here; both the Melos and the Amadeus, on the other hand, are very sensitive with it; but the most perceptive playing, I think, comes from the Aeolian Quartet, who throughout respond to the music's characteristic mixture of brightness and melancholy. The cello pizzicato bass looks like little more than a picking out of harmony notes; but the Aeolians' extra cellist, Bruno Schrecker, finds beautiful phrasing for this melody, as he makes it, to add an extra dimension to the music. I find this Quartet rather less effective when the melancholy of that opening projects the violent F minor middle section, and the recording could be cleaner. The Juilliard Quartet are properly vehement here, but a better balance with the opening is maintained by the Amadeus Quartet; and even better than the Amadeus are the Melos Quartet of Stuttgart with Rostropovich. They relate the power of this section to the opening, and charge it with passionate energy without losing control of its intricate textures, while Rostropovich underpins the whole in powerful triplets.

Schubert's Scherzo produces another contrast that needs very careful musical handling, for out of its vigorous C major stamping suddenly comes a Trio, marked *andante sostenuto*, in a very remote and startling key; it is an extraordinary passage, though one that is breathtakingly right for all that Schubert is doing in the work. With the confrontation as harsh, and shocking, as this, the ensemble which comes into its own is the Juilliard. They grasp the point of the music well, especially since this kind of abruptness and forcefulness is of the essence of their performance, rather too steadily and inflexibly so in other parts of the work. The other ensemble who bring this off particularly well are the Melos of Stuttgart, and though their style is less openly energetic than the Juilliard's they have a very sound grasp of the balance between the *presto* Scherzo and the *andante* Trio, and of how this is a different kind of contrast to the other confrontations in the work.

The Finale is, at any rate initially, much lighter, even rather disconcertingly so. Johann Mayrhofer found in Schubert a mixture of melancholy and sociability, and the suddenness with which he can turn aside from an intense experience into a conversational tone of pure charm is sometimes bewildering. The cheerfulness with which the Finale opens seems almost too light for all that has gone before, yet the tune which quickly follows it is even more lilting and sunny, as is shown by the Amadeus. They bring this off best of all the ensembles mentioned, and I think this is because they choose a tempo that allows for a touch of wistfulness.

The Amadeus performance is very sympathetic throughout, and though it is now twelve years old, it has earned its place in the catalogue and its claim on listeners' affections. I think it preferable to the somewhat harddriven Juilliard performance, which is also rather thinly recorded, and in another way preferable to the Lansdowne performance, which is scrupulous and clear but a little under-characterized. The Aeolian Quartet with Bruno Schrecker on a Saga record issued in 1966 is very good indeed, sometimes touching on the heart of the work more effectively than any of the others, but the recording has its defects and cannot really do justice to some of Schubert's imaginative scoring in the way that the others can. Nevertheless, it is a beautiful performance, and at the cheapest price of the lot, it is very good value indeed. However, probably the best all-round version is the one by the Melos Quartet of Stuttgart with Rostropovich. They respond to the music's energy and brightness, but they keep this in true balance with the melancholy and darkness and strangeness that are equally part of the character of this astonishing work. Even in the last bars, Schubert is disturbing the security of his C major with the D flat that made the key-contrast in the Scherzo and Trio, and there remains something equivocal in the dying away of the final unison C. It is the appreciation of these kind of points that lifts the Melos performance beyond the excellent into the exceptional.

Recordings Discussed

Stern Quartet/Tortelier	CBS 61043 (mono)
Vienna Philharmonic Quartet/Harand	Decca SDD 376
Amadeus Quartet/Pleeth	Deutsche Grammophon 139 105

Aeolian Quartet/Schrecker	Saga 5266
Tatrai Quartet/Szilvasy	Hungaroton SLPX 11611
Lansdowne Quartet/Fleming	WRC WRS 1005
Weller Quartet/Gurtler	Decca SDD 441
Alberni Quartet/Igloi	CRD 1018
Juilliard Quartet/Greenhouse	CBS 76268
*Melos Quartet of Stuttgart/Rostropovich	Deutsche Grammophon 2530 980

© John Warrack

Bach   Sonatas and Partitas for Solo Violin

ROBERT DONINGTON

In some ways these sonatas and partitas for unaccompanied violin are a remarkable kind of music. To take an instrument of melody not ordinarily intended to be heard by itself and to compose for it six long pieces in several movements, not to mention the repeats, is indeed a deliberate challenge. The sound of the violin can of course be varied; but only up to a point. The harmony can partly be sketched in by a lot of difficult double-stopping, multiple stopping actually; but there is a limit where the violinist runs out of fingers, and the violin runs out of strings. Whole passages have no chords at all except in so far as your mind picks them up from the outlines of the melody. Yet within these deliberate limitations a rich world builds up, a full world; and I somehow do not think that this particular world could have been built up in any other way.

Now this is obviously not music which is going to yield all its secrets at a few isolated hearings. No really concentrated music can, I suppose; but this unaccompanied violin music does rather go the limit for concentration. All the more worth adding it to your record collection, however, because the pleasure of living with it can become so very great. But also all the more important to choose a satisfactory performance: the challenge to the listener is to catch the pattern and fill out the meaning from this sparse flow of notes; but the challenge to the performer is to make it possible to do that. Every phrase and every articulation has to be moulded so that you can understand it; and every tempo has to be felt as the music wants it. You could say that it is difficult music to understand, but that when the player understands it he can get it across to you. It is not in any sense baffling music, and it comes to feel uncommonly natural music. But you do need a satisfactory performance.

Of the eight recorded performances, it seems to me that not one is without great merits of technique and musicianship and sheer beauty of violin sound. But I would not say that all of them are satisfactory. Salvatore Accardo, for example, is very impressive; but also to my feeling he is often slow. The overall effect is heavy; it is literal; it is remorseless; it is also too resonantly recorded. In short, it is – but again, simply to my feeling – a very good example of how not to do it. I should say, speaking violinistically, that it has all the virtues except the virtue of being right for Bach. On the other hand a very different violinist is Sergiu Luca. I do not think that his performance has all the virtues; but I do think that basically it is right for Bach. There is certainly an extraordinary difference between Accardo and Luca. I would, in fact, have hardly thought it possible that there could be so many different interpretations as one finds on these eight recordings, but of course if once you are off the right way . . . well anyhow, Luca certainly gives my idea of the right way, or should I say one right way, because I am sure that there is a good deal of choice possible within the boundaries of the style. But let me just suggest a few points. First of all, Luca's tempos are good, and that really does come first. He is never too slow. Second, his mood is quieter and more relaxed; that goes with the more lilting tempo. The music flows along so much more naturally like that. And here we come to what I think is the beginning of wisdom over these celebrated pieces. In a way, they are very big music: none bigger. But that is not the way in which to perform them. The bigger you try to make them, the less they go for. They get bogged down then with all that portentousness and weight. It becomes an awful strain, for example, listening to every full chord held remorselessly down, which can only be done on the violin by exerting the utmost pressure of the bow. Bach's own players never did that: we know from historical evidence that they just took it easy, and this is what Luca does. It is just that the big virtuoso style which was right for Brahms and Tchaikovsky will not work out very well for Bach; and this is the main difference between Accardo and Luca.

But there is another point to be considered. Just because we may want to get rather nearer to the way it used to be played in Bach's own day, we don't in the least have to do without all that virtuoso glory which came down into the nineteenth century by way of Viotti, who got it in the direct line from the great violinists of Bach's own day, like Geminiani and Tartini and Leopold Mozart; and behind them stands Corelli, of whom one of his own contemporaries wrote that 'I never met with any man that suffered his passions to hurry him away so much whilst he was playing on the violin as the famous Arcangelo Corelli . . . he gives in so much to what he is doing that he doth not look like the same man'. Well, you may possibly feel as I do, when listening to Luca's playing, that he doth not give in quite enough to what he is doing, and that he might with advantage have suffered his passions to hurry him away just that much more. Still, both for style and for sound I would rate his performances very high; and as to the sound, I should certainly point out that the very beautiful Amati violin which Luca uses has had its internal fittings put back from the usual modernized state into their original state. That gives a less massive sound, and clearer, and of course it does go better with Bach's music, which he composed with just that lighter original violin sound in mind. By the way, you will notice that the pitch is a semitone down. It is supposed to be Bach's pitch, but in fact that is a bit of a gimmick, because pitch then was variable anyhow. If Luca has weaknesses, the fugue in the First Sonata, for example, sounds to me just a bit too light, and a little sluggish, and even a little mannered – which is certainly not an authentic feature.

Now it is quite possible to have an approach to Bach which is not very authentic but not very nineteenth-century either. I do not myself think that Josef Suk is entirely acceptable: his playing is crisper than Accardo, but his Sarabande from the First Partita sounds distinctly ponderous, and the Bourrée from the same Partita is graceless and really 'hacked out', perhaps Sandor Végh on Telefunken is another case of what I would call in this connection a good conventional interpreter. He is more relaxed than either Accardo or Suk, too much relaxed at times, for example in the opening *grave* of the Second Sonata, which strikes me as, if anything, a little flabby and says practically nothing to me, I am afraid. Very sincere playing, of course, but fairly clueless. And perhaps the recording is to blame for this, but it actually sounds a little thin and spidery. On the other hand I find Végh's rendering of the Gavotte from the E major Partita, a bit lightweight, yet it suits this movement and I find it delightful.

All this just goes to show that you cannot expect the same violinist to be equally good in so many extremely varied movements. Bratislav Novotny on Supraphon is another violinist who is very good in many parts, and by no means inclined to kill by kindness. I mean by this that he does not overload the sound, and he does allow the music to ripple along in a natural kind of way. Not boring, on the one hand, and not pretentious, on the other, he is at his best in the really rather jolly little *presto* which ends the First Sonata. Not that this is one of the more difficult movements to phrase correctly provided you are willing just to let it ripple along. Nevertheless, it is possible to make rather more of it, in fact quite a lot more, as Menuhin does. It is the glorious vitality of Menuhin's performance which pleases me. The sheer joy of the music is so essential in good Bach playing. Nathan Milstein has the same kind of joy, so to speak in a more lightweight conception. The way he opens the Preludio to the E major Partita is a good illustration, with its impulsive flow of notes.

I find Milstein very good indeed, and his is altogether an excellent recording, only perhaps just lacking for me the last refinement of poetry and of warmth. But really for lack of poetry and warmth you have to hear Heifetz, such a superlative violinist in his own steely perfection, though I have never been one of those who liked his style, and perhaps least of all in Bach. I would not quite say that he gives us the soulless perfection of the machine, but his playing gives me almost that sort of inhuman feeling, and I am bound to say I dislike it very much, especially in the slow movements. It is Menuhin, I think, who has most got what it takes, and the best test is the famous Chaconne in D minor in the Second Partita. Personally I think Luca is also pretty marvellous here: there is no weakness in his performance of this piece at all. It is big enough playing in all conscience; but it is done by simply letting the music come through in its natural shapes and patterns – no mean achievement in musical understanding, mind you, and how easy he makes it on the listener. And the sound of that baroque fiddle – out of this world, and of course *into* the world of Bach. The only rival to Luca here is Menuhin. There are some passages which I feel are on the heavy side; but then I am greatly wedded to the lighter, sharper manner for any baroque violin music, Bach's included. For the rest, I feel quite carried away by this sense of glory which is brought out by the way Menuhin does that astonishing modulation to the major in the Chaconne – simple enough as a musical effect, but the feeling Menuhin puts into it and the beauty of his tone are one notch beyond anything that Luca or the others could do: a sudden depth of tragedy and intensity. It is more than just poetry and warmth. Glory is my word for it.

This is the kind of playing which makes me feel that Menuhin, remaining at his best, is the greatest of living violinists. So my choice of recording for the unaccompanied Violin Sonatas and Partitas lies between Menuhin, for his greatness and his glory in movement after movement, on the one hand; and Luca, for his closeness to Bach's own authentic style and sound, on the other hand. Both are well recorded, except that Menuhin's version has a bit too much resonance. There is great joy in both sets: Luca does sound so absolutely natural to the music, and Menuhin in a sense transcends it.

Recordings Discussed

Heifetz	RCA SER 5669–71
Suk	HMV CSD 3710–2
Menuhin	HMV SLS 5045
Milstein	Deutsche Grammophon 2709 047
Accardo	Philips 6703 076
Végh	Telefunken AS 6.35344
*Luca	Nonesuch HC 73030
Novotny	Supraphon 111 1101–3

Beethoven *Piano Sonata in B flat, Op.106, 'Hammerklavier'*

JEREMY SIEPMANN

Everything about the 'Hammerklavier' is difficult. It is famously difficult to play, not much easier to listen to, and it poses fairly formidable challenges as well to the comparative reviewer. Part of the problem is the sheer size of the piece: the average performance time only just falls short of fifty minutes. But length is the least of it. Every movement is an unprecedented kaleidoscope of emotions, ideas, and technical challenges, and the sum of the parts – each of which is a different phase of one cataclysmic experience – results in the most stupendous case of musical assault and battery I know of. We are confronted in the 'Hammerklavier' both with an unparalleled spiritual and intellectual exercise and with an act of Revolution which completely shattered the sound-world of the eighteenth century and paved the way not only for Chopin, Liszt, Schumann, and Brahms but also for Stravinsky, Bartók, and Messiaen. The ending of the last movement is a body-blow which must have terrified, even more than it enraged, most of Beethoven's contemporaries.

The 'Hammerklavier', more than most pieces, has to be experienced as a whole. And it is that – plus the fact that it covers more intellectual and emotional ground than can ever be revealed in one performance – which makes it such an intractable subject for this kind of comparison. Its universality alone makes me feel that any self-respecting record library should either contain several versions of the piece or none, and it is the last work in the world that one should ever risk 'getting used to'. Any listener (or any performer, for that matter) who 'knows how it goes' has become inaccessible to the music, (it is *not* the other way round). Take the first movement: of course it can be, as in Ashkenazy's performance, a challenge, followed by a knock-down, drag-out struggle. But it can also be conveyed as a monumental assertion, almost melancholy in its affirmation. This emerges clearly in the more spacious view of Wilhelm Backhaus. Again, it may be understood as the working-out of a Sphinx-like riddle, the challenge of an enigma: take Kempff's performance where the effect is achieved through a fairly liberal approach to Beethoven's markings. If, in fact, textual accuracy matters a lot to you then I think you can drop from your shopping-list not only Kempff but Arrau and even Barenboim as well. All of them take what you might call an intensely 'personal' approach, adapting the score (sometimes quite freely) to the demands of their temperaments at the time – 're-composing' the music, as it were, in the crucible of their own perceptions and intuitions. The problem here is that what sounds fresh and boldly exploratory in the concert hall can easily sound mannered and even distracting in the frozen world of the gramophone record.

With a view to living with one of them, you might compare the more purely 'interpretive' approach of Pollini, with the unashamedly 'creative' playing of Claudio Arrau. Kempff, Barenboim, and Arrau all bring to their playing the breadth and adventurousness, the sense of spontaneity (even of improvisation) which was for a long time the hallmark of the composer-pianist. Their personalities dominate their performances. If I say that Pollini and Ashkenazy are more self-effacing, that they approach the work more in the spirit of the museum curator, I am not suggesting for a moment that there is anything dead, or even dull, about their playing. But where Arrau, Barenboim, and Kempff rather flamboyantly put their virtuosity at the service of music, Pollini and Ashkenazy put *their* formidable powers more specifically at the service of Beethoven. The result, in each case, is a dazzling realization of the printed page.

The middle ground between what I shall call the Recreators and the Curators is occupied by Brendel (in two recordings), Serkin, Solomon, and Backhaus. Of these, Backhaus seems to commute most freely between the two camps. Despite occasional moments of, to me, unfathomable abandon, his performance is notable for its almost comfortable control. Backhaus, in fact, is one of the few pianists who leave one (or who leave me, at any rate) with an impression not so much of titanic struggle as of fist-shaking jubilation. Once the first movement is behind him, Solomon is another. There is, in his playing of the fugue, a kind of manic joy which, combined with an unusually long-lined approach to phrasing, may convince many listeners that this music is not only great but actually beautiful.

In striking contrast to Solomon's approach (which by the end suggests an almost serene recollection of past pain and struggle) is the performance of Rudolf Serkin, which has been re-released in a two-record set from CBS. For him there is nothing past about either the pain or the struggle. Either one must remain detached from his intense experience of the work or become exhaustingly involved in it. His battle with the elements is so immediate that almost from the outset it becomes irrelevant whether one 'likes' the performance or not. Even in the Scherzo, the only movement which approaches lightness, the tension is almost abrasive.

However, if there is too much tension for your taste in Serkin's playing, and perhaps too little in that of Solomon or Backhaus, you may find an acceptable blending of forces in the versions by Brendel, Ashkenazy, and Pollini, all of whom are in peak form. In fact, if you are approaching the 'Hammerklavier' for the first time, and if you are not already a card-carrying member of one of the other camps, I think you would do best to make your choice from these four. All the available versions contain first-rate playing but these seem to me the most consistent, and the freest from distracting idiosyncrasies. I must come back here and stress the point I made earlier: living with a gramophone record is an experience different in kind from that of the concert hall, and performances must be evaluated with that in mind.

Brendel's two readings strike me as being more 'personal' than those of Pollini or Ashkenazy, by which I mean that his projection of the score, so to speak, is less literal. Without the sometimes inconsequential eccentricities which, for me, mar the performances of Kempff and Arrau, Brendel seasons his playing with occasional liberties which balance his mastery with a sense of spontaneous reaction. It is interesting to compare his slightly 'orchestrated' approach (particularly in the opening of the sonata) with the very straight reading given by Pollini. Where Pollini plays exactly what is written, Brendel takes a slightly freer (and very subtle) approach to both rhythm and articulation and goes so far as to double the opening upbeat at the octave. If even that degree of what we might call 'instant transcription' seems excessive to you, then the field narrows further still, leaving us with Ashkenazy and Pollini. Pollini is perhaps the purer of the two, Ashkenazy communicating, to me anyway, a greater degree of personal involvement. But here – as with the whole batch – it is a wicked choice to have to make, and I can only repeat that, ideally, I would choose several or none.

If you are not already a devoted partisan of Arrau's my personal inclination is to suggest you look elsewhere. The playing is formidable, but I find it too idiosyncratic to be suitable for the caged life of a gramophone performance. The same goes for Kempff's where in addition to the omission of the first-movement repeat there is the infuriating necessity of turning the record over in the middle of the Adagio, so putting his version out of court. Barenboim does some deeply impressive playing, but there seems to me a disproportionate focus on secondary details which robs the piece of its necessary wholeness. Backhaus plays very well for the most part (though I am not always quite sure what he is up to), and Solomon suffers, if anything, from excessive mastery; but the recordings are old – and in any case, if you are a devotee of either player their versions are probably already in your collection.

For me the most involving performance is Serkin's, but, like Arrau's, which it otherwise scarcely resembles, it is perhaps too big, too personal, too powerful, to live happily in a domestic record library. Thus, reluctantly, I must pass it by and come to what seem to me the most successful gramophone performances. These are by Brendel (whose Philips version also gives you the Op. 78 Sonata) Pollini, And Ashkenazy.

Forced to a final choice – and using the criteria which I suggested earlier – I think I should have to opt for Pollini. His long-limbed, sinewy almost ascetic performance combines exemplary musicianship with superb pianism and the lack of anything which could irritate or distract the listener – on first or repeated hearings.

Recordings Discussed

Kempff	Deutsche Grammophon 2539 329
Solomon	HMV RLS 722 (part of 7-record set)
Brendel (1963)	Turnabout TV 34112S
Arrau	Philips 6747 009 (part of 13-record set)
*Ashkenazy	Decca SXL 6335
Barenboim	HMV SLS 794 (part of 12-record set)
Backhaus	Decca SXLA 6452-61 (part of 10-record set)
*Brendel (1972)	Philips 6500 139
Serkin	CBS 79004 (2-record set)
*Pollini	Deutsche Grammophon 2530 869

© Jeremy Siepmann

Mozart   *Piano Sonata in A, K331*

JEREMY SIEPMANN

Some time ago I found myself in Leeds. Now I realize that that may strike you
as an almost abrasively irrelevant confession to make but it is, in fact, very
much to the point because my experience in Yorkshire had a fairly
fundamental effect on my approach to the present comparison. I was there,
on behalf of the BBC, as an observer of the Leeds International Piano
Competition, and in the course of my observing I underwent, in a dis-
turbingly intensified form, an experience which regular listeners to
'Building a Library' are used to getting, in spoon-size doses, almost every
week. Well I was getting it, day by day, not by the pint even, but by the
gallon – and I began to wonder whether my professional critical faculties
were being unhinged or set ever more firmly, and healthily, on the rails. I
was being subjected, voluntarily (or at least under contract) to successive
performances of one piece by a variety of different players. I was not alone,
of course. There was a regular audience, and there was the jury, made up of
highly professional musicians from all over the world. What was
confronting us all, particularly those of us who were professionals, was far
more important, and far more troubling, than the spectacle of young
pianists confronting Art in a competitive arena invaded by Ladbroke's.
What was confronting us was the very nature of musical experience itself.
How do we listen? And why? And how is our listening affected by the
environment and context in which we experience it?

Now if you should be thinking that the pondering of these questions is
solely the prerogative of musical philosophers then I suggest, with all due
respect, that my final choice of performance of this sonata will probably be
immaterial to you. In fact I am not at all sure that I don't think it is, and
should be, immaterial – to all of us. In my exploration of the available
versions of Mozart's A major Sonata, I shall try and explain, defend, and
disarm, that apparently self-defeating statement. In the process I shall also
hope to make your choice easier.

The opening theme of the first movement is said to be one of the reasons
why this is Mozart's most popular sonata. Is it Mozart's most popular sonata?
I don't think it is among *pianists*, but with audiences it well may be,
particularly the last movement, the famous Rondo alla turca. Without
meaning to disparage either the sonata or the public, I would suggest that

the piece owes its popularity not only to the grace and easy beauty which permeate it, but to the fact that it is a particularly straightforward, uncomplicated and relatively undemanding work. I think it must be a symptom of its straightforwardness that there is a really very striking similarity between most of the available recorded versions, despite the fact that they come from pianists who are by no means all of a kind: Backhaus, Solomon, Brendel, Klien, Kempff, Alicia de Larrocha and the Russian-born Czech pianist Valentina Kameníková. The plain, and for our purposes rather inconvenient fact, is that they are all very well played and I could recommend the lot of them quite happily. Yet surely I must have some preference, and, in fact, I have. For me, one version stands out from all the others (and I shall duly recommend it at the end) but that does not alter the fact that they are all good, and mostly, as I have said, remarkably alike. If you have very strong feelings about the way this piece should go, you probably play it yourself and have no interest in adding it to your record library. If you do not, you will probably base any decision to buy or not to buy (which is, of course, the question) on the couplings, rather than on the basis of this sonata itself. If you have no very strong feelings about this particular sonata but have very decided ideas about the way Mozart should be played, you probably will not be prepared to settle for an approach like Kempff's. His playing may at times sound a little suggestive of Brahms, but in the context of the creative insights which characterize the whole performance I cannot say it troubles me very much. I liked his performance very much indeed when I first heard it, as did a professional colleague who was listening with me. She is, by the way, a performer of the piece herself. A few days later we both listened again. I then found it rather strident in sound and irritating in mannerism, but I kept this to myself until my companion said, 'I don't like this very much at all, do you?' 'No', I admitted, 'but it's the same performance we both loved the other day.' And here were two seasoned professionals. Beware hard and fast judgements for the Muse is fickle and mercurial. Three days later I heard Kempff again and liked his performance very much, though not perhaps, quite so much as the first time. What had happened? Different days, different moods, yes; but something else too, something which is at the heart of my reluctance to juxtapose two performances of the same passage. On that second occasion, when neither of us had liked it, we had not listened to it on its own – as we had done the first time – but immediately following Walter Klien's performance.

The problem was the same as that which bore down so hard on me in Leeds when two or more pianists in succession played the same movement from the same piece. The fact is, I think, that what is true for the performer is also true for the listener, namely that context alters content. The problem with Kempff on that second occasion was that we were listening to him in a context already prejudiced, in the purest sense of the word, by our still-fresh memory of Klien. And there is another curious fact, which strengthened still more my determination to avoid close juxtapositions of examples. My impression that the basic approach of virtually all the players was strikingly similar was based on separated hearings of the whole sonata, during which I defended myself from the vagaries of memory by taking notes and marking the score. Later I listened through once again to the whole lot – this time without making or consulting notes and with the performances in a different order. My impression of unanimity remained, but when I came to make close comparisons – phrase with phrase, so to speak – I found far greater discrepancies than I expected, both in tempo and emphasis.

Without the possibility of presenting all the performances in their entirety, how could I convey an accurate impression of each interpretation if the parts by themselves seemed to me to create a false picture of the whole? Well, in some cases I obviously was not. Where there were deviations from what we might call the stylistic norm and where these might threaten, after repeated hearings, to become irritating mannerisms, I should obviously have to be unfair to the performer in order to give fair notice to the potential buyer. Backhaus, for instance, has a tendency to let the metre swirl into occasional eddies which could prove distracting. For all that there is much I admire and like in Backhaus's playing, his slightly slippery grip on the metre and the somewhat antiquated recorded sound put his version out of court, at least as a candidate for anybody's first choice. Solomon's recording too suffers a little from technological old age but the piano-playing is always beautiful, the style appropriately lyrical without being romantic, and there are no excesses of any kind. It is not what you might call a sharply high-lighted performance (he tends to underplay small-scale contrasts in favour of larger ones), but the sonata emerges with exemplary charm and elegance.

Walter Klien's performance is slightly sharper-edged than Solomon's, and more recently recorded too, but I find it in no way less beautiful. He combines a fairly scrupulous attention to the eighteenth-century text with a sometimes almost lushly nineteenth-century approach to his instrument. The sound is rounded, and the pedal more generously used than might be approved of by certain musicological scolds, but, for an eclectic and romantic twentieth-century puritan like me, the combination works beautifully. If there are shades of impressionist mist surrounding the Trio section in the second movement, I am not one to get steamed up about it. Throughout the sonata, Klein maintains the same basic approach: beautiful sounds, an evenly balanced deployment of contrasts, and expressive inflections. Now, although I feel that most of the pianists take a roughly similar view of the piece, there are two quite notable exceptions, and they are (in this case) distinguished representatives of opposing views. One is Valentina Kameniková, the other is Alfred Brendel. With a very sparing and deliberately plotted use of contrasts, Brendel manages to unify the whole work in a way I have not heard done before, and he counters the stereotype notion of the piece (as a charming and lively but ultimately rather shallow piece of art and artifice) with the suggestion, implicit in his tempos, articulation, and sometimes rather ascetic sound that, on the contrary, it is a far more serious statement than we tend to take it for.

Valentina Kameniková provides the most kaleidoscopic performance of the lot. There is no point in my making any secret of it; out of an excellent batch of recordings by masterful artists who know just what they are doing, this one leaps into first place with unexpected ease. Valentina Kameniková does not play the piece in the way I would, but she brings to her highly characterful performance (which, by the way never approaches quirkiness) most of the qualities which I find most central to the making of music. One of these is variety, which of course is an easily abusable commodity. Another is consequence. In fact let me refine them into a single virtue: variety born of consequence. E. M. Forster once very succinctly described what for him was the difference between a story and a plot. 'The king died; the queen died', he said, 'that is a story'. 'The king died; the queen died of heartbreak. That is a plot.' In music, no less than in novels, the queen must die of something. Things do not merely happen: they result from other things. It is this sense of continuous consequence, of the quicksilver action and reaction of musical elements, more than the superb piano-playing or the excellent recorded sound which, for me, put Kameniková's record way out front. My admiration and deep-felt respect for the other players remains. They are all artists who know their way and they all play well, but only Kameniková breathes quite so much life into the piece. She has surprised me by convincing me that the A major sonata is better than I had ever thought it, not merely an excellent and delightful piece but a downright wonderful one. Even if one was not aware of the fact, one could well guess from this masterly, bright, and dramatic piano-playing that Mozart was, as he remains, the greatest, and subtlest, of all operatic composers.

But now we hit the snags. I have left little room for doubt that Kameniková is my first choice. But she may not be yours, and even if she is, you may be deterred by the fact that the coupling in this case gives you only one more piece, the F major sonata, K332, whereas most of the others offer more. For instance, the Klien/Turnabout version gives you two other sonatas. With Brendel you get one extra, K333, and the B minor Adagio. Solomon gets you another sonata and the C minor Concerto. Larrocha gives you more Mozart and the Bach-Busoni Chaconne. And so it goes. I suppose the choice depends partly on whether you are more interested in the menu than the meal. Well I have made *my* choice, but the plain fact is that beyond a few essentials there are no absolutes in music and the choice has got to boil down, in the end, to personal taste and one's own particular character. It is as simple as that.

Recordings Discussed

Solomon	HMV RLS 726
Backhaus	Decca ECS 749
Kempff	Deutsche Grammophon 2535 168
Klien (1965)	Turnabout TV 34504S
Klien (1971)	Turnabout 37004S
Larrocha	Decca SXL 6669
*Kameniková	Supraphon 111 1417
Brendel	Philips 9500 025

© Jeremy Siepmann

Schumann   *Liederkreis, Op. 39*

J. W. LAMBERT

Schumann was rising thirty when he suddenly found that notes alone were
not enough to express his passionate feelings – mixed feelings as always,
although his tumultuous love for the famous young pianist Clara Wieck was
approaching a happy issue out of all its afflictions. At the beginning of 1840
he found himself pouring out song after song: 'I've composed so much it
almost frightens me; but I can't help it.' He formed many of the songs – or
they formed themselves – into groups, which he referred to indifferently as
Kreise (*Kreis* is a vague sort of word with circular connotations) or as
cycles: the Heine settings of Op.24, the bran-tub of twenty-six songs
gathered in *Myrthen*, the twelve songs of Op.39 (*Liederkreis*, written at
more or less the same time as the further Heine settings in the
Dichterliebe), and then of course *Frauenliebe und -leben*.

The Op. 39 songs are all settings of Eichendorff, a German romantic,
but not a frenzied one. His verse appealed to Schumann's dual personality
through its mixture of the rapturous and the foreboding, its celebration of
the beauty of the natural world threatened by dark, destructive forces, and
of the potential glory of human love at the mercy of time, separation, and
betrayal. These are the essential subjects of the twelve songs.

Of the six versions available on record at the moment, two are by
sopranos, two by mezzos, one by a tenor, one by a baritone. I should say for
a start that I am not bothered by the fact that two of the songs speak a man's
thoughts, at least one of them a woman's. The emotions expressed are
common to both sexes. Nor can I fuss about transpositions. All will be well,
provided that singer and pianist (for of course these are duets, not solos with
piano accompaniment) can achieve the temperamental unity underlying the
changes of mood. No less essential, they must avoid an inner monotony on
the one hand, and breaking the sequence into individual numbers on the
other. Success or failure in that respect cannot be demonstrated in a short
review, but I hope you will be able to draw your own conclusions, which
may or may not agree with mine, if I try to illustrate what seem to me
characteristic qualities of these six interpreters, or rather six pairs of
interpreters, though I must regretfully eliminate the most recently issued of
these recordings, from Erato. Birgit Finnalä is a mezzo soprano with strong,
clear projection and an evident sense of drama; but her pianist, Rudolf

Jansen, gets rather heavily-handed on his Steinway, and she herself all too often slides into a ruinously whining tone.

The *Liederkreis* originally began with a jolly song, 'Der frohe Wandersmann'; but Schumann had second thoughts, and replaced it with 'In der Fremde', an evocation of exile and resignation. Perhaps he thought it seemed more tactful not to seem too chirpy to the absent Clara. Already forgotten in the lost homeland, the singer reflects that, wherever it may be, the peace of death will soon bring oblivion anyway. Janet Baker, with Daniel Barenboim, beginning I must say as she means to go on, surprisingly strikes me as sounding positively querulous rather than regretfully resigned; Elisabeth Schwarzkopf and Geoffrey Parsons, on the other hand, are rather more in the mood of the song.

The next song, 'Intermezzo', is clearly addressed straight to Clara. It is a piquantly syncopated rêverie of delight at the thought of the loved one, and I do like the way Schwarzkopf catches the youthful eagerness as well as the yearning. But in the next song she takes a very different turn. 'Waldesgespräch' is a short ballad. A cheerful young man, riding through the woods, meets a beautiful woman, is warned off, tries again, and suddenly realizes that she is that fatal creature the Lorelei, who finally tells him forcibly that he is never going to get out of the wood. Schwarzkopf does more than that. She turns the beautiful cold creature suddenly into an almost visible old crone. Fischer-Dieskau, with Christoph Eschenbach, you will find, does not dramatize as much as that, but he does vividly catch the young rider's moment of horrified recognition.

Though the encounters of humanity with the dark forces of nature is a theme running through the whole *Liederkreis*, this song is its only overtly dramatic expression. After it comes 'Die Stille', about a girl thinking of her man. The singer is sitting snug at home one winter night dreaming of the beloved, but has a sudden fancy that it would be marvellous to be a bird and fly up and away. In this song I greatly like the fresh youthfulness of Jessye Norman on Philips. As for the men, Robert Tear, with Philip Ledger, is breezily uninhibited about it all. There's no danger of *him* getting too whimsical, and his is an effective way of avoiding a potentially awkward moment. In the next song, the justly celebrated 'Mondnacht', though, all but one of the singers insist on making things difficult for themselves by taking it exceedingly slowly. Irwin Gage, Jessye Norman's pianist, for example has trouble with the repeated chords in 'Mondnacht's' last two taxing verses. It would be fine, I dare say, with Norman's inspiring presence on the concert platform; but it is too extended for the isolation of the record. After all, 'Mondnacht' is not even marked 'slow', let alone 'very slow', only 'delicately', 'with a sense of mystery'. Fischer-Dieskau's easy pace seems to me to capture the magic more successfully than if all the linked sweetness is too long drawn out. Yet when it comes to expressing the joyful certainty that something splendid is going to happen in 'Schöne Fremde' Jessye Norman's freshness really shows its worth.

Though it is not open to analysis, there is no missing Jessye Norman's surging vitality. Janet Baker tries to achieve the effect by taking the song very fast: but it is marked to be sung 'inwardly', and I cannot say it sounds like that to me. In fact Dame Janet's interpretation as a whole seems to me to have about it a certain matter-of-factness, not to say impatience; and at least on her record there is not much bloom on the voice. In another song with the same title as the first, 'In der Fremde', a lover, amidst all the beauties of nature, can almost believe that the beloved is waiting – but the beloved is long since dead; here I am afraid even the last two verses, more touching than the first two, sound to me more like bald statements than yearning evocations. I find the same thing, too, in 'Wehmut', a song which epitomizes what Shakespeare's Jessica meant when she said 'I am never merry when I hear sweet music'.

I find especially puzzling, and uncomfortably revealing, a too extreme approach, which, whatever the actual speed they adopt, all but Schwarzkopf and Fischer-Dieskau seem to bring to 'Auf einer Berg' that eerie vision of a crumbling statue in a ruined castle looking down upon a wedding party and a weeping bride. Or consider 'Zwielicht', 'twilight' – a very different twilight from the one in 'Schöne Fremde'. This is an extraordinarily bitter statement of human frailty. If you have a friend, don't trust him. There is always tomorrow, it's true, but much can be lost by night – watch out! Schwarzkopf has the measure of it, especially in the way she colours 'Morgen' and 'Neugeboren', draining the words of hope. But Schumann was not going to end these particular offerings to Clara on a gloomy note, whatever his earlier misgivings. He brought the *Liederkreis* to a radiant close with 'Frühlingsnacht', in which all Nature conspires to assure him that 'she is thine, she is thine!' I find that all six singers take wing in this one, though Robert Tear does rather seem to be exulting not so much with a smile as through bared teeth, in a rather predatory and possessive way.

To sum up, I must express disappointment with Janet Baker's to me unsympathetic handling of the songs (HMV). In many of them I am strongly drawn to Jessye Norman for her freshness and buoyancy (Philips). But though Elizabeth Schwarzkopf (HMV) may be past her prime simply as a vocalist she seems often to turn even difficulties to expressive advantage, and has the songs in her very bones, so that she here seems less self-conscious than often in the past. Of the two men Robert Tear offers an enjoyable, lively, fresh young fellow, ready to sing away his misgivings; hearty might be too strong a word, but not much (Argo). Fischer-Dieskau uses his lightest voice (DG). The mannerisms which irritate some people are almost entirely absent, though Christoph Eschenbach, I do feel, is sometimes a touch finicky in his piano figures. Yet their partnership draws richness from every song. So my first choice must be for Schwarzkopf with Geoffrey Parsons, and for Fischer-Dieskau, with Eschenbach.

Recordings Discussed

Tear/Ledger	Argo ZRG 718
Baker/Barenboim	HMV ASD 3217
Schwarzkopf/Parsons	HMV ASD 3037
Fischer-Dieskau/Eschenbach	Deutsche Grammophon 2563 781
Norman/Gage	Philips 9500 110
Finnalä/Jansen	Erato STU 71155

Arnold Bax

ANDREW KEENER

This review is primarily an introduction to the records of a composer who still attracts a lot of criticism. Bax's ideas are attractive, it is reluctantly admitted, but they are not developed strongly enough to sustain the length of much of his music. At one time, of course, people said that about Mahler and Rakhmaninov, to name just two composers who have since prompted second thoughts. I propose to suggest some recordings for anyone coming to Bax for the first time, and perhaps in the process we shall became aware that he deserves second thoughts as well. But what of the smaller-scale Bax? After all, he was Master of the King's and then the Queen's Music until his death in 1953, and there is no doubt that he was fully capable of pomp and circumstance when the occasion demanded, as in the Coronation March of 1953, played by the London Symphony Orchestra and conducted by Sir Malcolm Sargent on a record available in electronic stereo on Decca's 'Eclipse' label (ECS 649). The fact that Bax's few ceremonial compositions seldom ring true offers some clue to his very inward-looking character. Unlike Elgar, for example, Bax was rarely inspired by man-made ceremony, though he was responsive to the splendour of the natural world. Indeed, the two men's lives seem to have moved in opposite directions. While Elgar was the son of a simple music-shop owner, late in life to become a socially-accepted patriot, Bax, from comfortable middle-class surroundings, ended his days introspectively in rented lodgings. The composer who wrote 'Finished, thank God'! at the end of his 1937 Coronation March was revealing his true self in music such as his Symphonic Poem *Tintagel*, behind which lurks the phantom of Debussy's *La Mer*; not for nothing was Bax one of the many to fall under that spell. As a young man he was fascinated by the Atlantic, whether he was viewing it from the remote twilight of Western Ireland or, as in *Tintagel*, from the castle on Cornwall's coastline. Here we find bold, vigorous tone-painting which requires equally vivid performance; and little, I think, is to be gained by underplaying these qualities. The horn writing, in particular, is some of the most exciting in late Romantic music. *Tintagel* makes an excellent start to any Bax collection, and there are two fine stereo performances in the current catalogue, one by Sir Adrian Boult with the London Philharmonic Orchestra on Lyrita, and the other with Sir John Barbirolli and the London

Symphony Orchestra on HMV. After the majestic opening comes a middle section which recalls the legends evoked by the ruined castle. A restless melody, high on cellos, introduces an episode during which echoes of Wagner's *Tristan* can be heard, first on solo violin and oboe, and later from several sections of the orchestra. The first point to note in Sir Adrian Boult's recording is the superb orchestral definition achieved by conductor and recording engineers. The clarity of the tuba and string basses is excellent, the separated first and second violins open out the texture splendidly, and Boult's grading of tension and speed is most impressive. The record also contains *The Garden of Fand*, the first *Northern Ballad*, and *Mediterranean*, a delightfully bogus picture-postcard from a holiday in Spain (Lyrita SRCS 62).

Now to Barbirolli's *Tintagel* on HMV. As you would expect from a master of the instrument, the cello melody is savoured lovingly and the harp accompaniment comes over as a richer if rather hazier wash of sound than with the Boult. But the most marked difference occurs when the music becomes restless, and here Barbirolli has the marking in the score on his side; in his performance the music surges forward, making the most of the sudden crescendos and diminuendos, and there is some magnificent horn-playing. So the choice between Boult's comparative restraint and Barbirolli's impulsiveness must be personal; for me it is Barbirolli who presents the full sensation of sunlight on lashing spray, and the mighty strength of the sea. His record is coupled with pieces by John Ireland and Delius, a less useful compendium for the Bax collector, but worth its price for *Tintagel* alone (HMV ASD 2305.)

The years during and after the First War were troubled ones for Bax; the Easter Rising had robbed him of several friends, he had been refused service on grounds of health, and then he had domestic trouble and his father's death to cope with. The ivory tower of his youth, to use his own words in describing his former security, had crumbled. Out of this came the First Symphony, written in 1921, and available in a fine recording by the London Philharmonic Orchestra conducted by Myer Fredman on Lyrita. It is one of those strange musical coincidences that both Bax and Sibelius wrote seven symphonies; Bax dedicated his Fifth to the Finnish master, and although their musical personalities were hardly similar, the two composers possessed a symphonic style that was highly personal. In fact, Bax's working out of ideas frequently possesses a Sibelian concentration as in the First Symphony, a tense, angry work Lyrita SRCS 53).

Lyrita's engineering in their Bax recordings is impressively natural, almost as if, once a satisfactory balance had been struck, no further work at the mixing desk was necessary, although this surely underestimates the work that must have been put into these recordings. So it is rather a pity to realize that the last symphony to appear in this series became available in 1975. To complete them on record, it would be good to think that Vernon Handley was about to be asked to give us No. 4, as he did in the early '60s with the (then amateur) Guildford Philharmonic Orchestra, deleted many years ago now.

And so on to 1928 and 1929, important years in Bax's life, during which he was slowly regaining something of his former composure, shifting the source of his inspiration from the western twilight of Ireland to the hardly less evocative Morar in Scotland. This move prompted the Third Symphony and the Third Piano Sonata, and in them both we glimpse several of the characteristics of the mature Bax. Both works have dark, sombre openings which hover around the minor third in a way peculiar to the composer. The Sonata is beautifully played on an adequate sounding mono Lyrita record (RCS 12) by Iris Loveridge and it demonstrates how the ruminative opening theme can become a very much more determined affair simply by applying a driving rhythm to it – a favourite device with Bax. The Sonata is a fine piece and well worth exploring; yet how much more convincing those devices employed in the Sonata become on moving to the richer possibilities of the Third Symphony where Bax can give free rein to the orchestral thinking that must have been behind works such as the Sonata. The opening minor third has the same sombre feeling about it, while the transformation of the theme into an energetic rhythm is far more expertly managed. The Third, probably Bax's finest and most accessible symphony, is available at mid-price, played by the London Symphony Orchestra conducted by Edward Downes, with some fine playing, especially from the brass. The symphony ends with an Epilogue, a device much favoured by British composers, including Vaughan Williams. Rather than being attached to the end of the Finale, Bax's Epilogue is not a self-contained section, but gradually winds down the main theme of the movement; the same kind of thinking that prompted Elgar in the transition from Scherzo to slow movement in his First Symphony is also at work here – not so ingeniously, but nevertheless prompted by the same spirit. The record comes from RCA on GL 42247 at medium price.

It would be difficult to imagine such broad serenity as one finds at the end of the Third Symphony working potently in chamber music. It is perhaps appropriate, then, if rather a pity, that chamber music is the area of Bax's output least well represented in the current catalogue. I for one would willingly exchange the Trio for Flute, Viola, and Harp, sensitively played as it is, by the Robles Trio on Argo for the Piano Quintet, cast in the same tough mould as the First Symphony. The Quintet is also one of the few chamber works which seems able to accommodate Bax's lush orchestral thinking without bursting at the seams. However, I must finally recommend the Legend Sonata for Cello and Piano, written eight years before the composer's death. It has a certain easy contentment about it, while there is no suspicion of any attempt to compress orchestral textures into a medium too small for them. If you know the cello sonata of Bax's friend John Ireland, then the parallel here with its Finale is rather striking, both in general mood and in the resemblance of the main themes, a rapid flick of a tune which cheekily doubles back on itself. Florence Hooton, the Sonata's dedicatee, who knew both Bax and Ireland, is the excellent cellist though it is a pity she and her pianist Wilfrid Parry sound as if they recorded it in a broom cupboard. (Lyrita RCS 6 mono).

Recordings of Works Discussed

Coronation March. London Symphony Orchestra/Sargent	Decca ECS 649
Legend-Sonata for cello and piano. Hooton/Parry	Lyrita RCS 6 (mono)
Mediterranean. London Philharmonic Orchestra/Boult	Lyrita SRCS 62
Northern Ballad. London Philharmonic Orchestra/Boult	Lyrita SRCS 62
Sonata No. 3 for piano. Loveridge	Lyrita RCS 12 (mono)
Symphony No.1. London Philharmonic Orchestra/ Fredman	Lyrita SRCS 53
Symphony No.3. London Symphony Orchestra/Downes	RCA GL 42247
The Garden of Fand. London Philharmonic Orchestra/ Boult	Lyrita SRCS 62
Tintagel. London Symphony Orchestra/Barbirolli	HMV ASD 2305
Tintagel. London Philharmonic Orchestra/Boult	Lyrita SRCS 62
Trio (Elegy) for flute, viola, and harp. Robles Trio	Argo ZRG 574

© Andrew Keener

Berkeley on Record

CHRISTOPHER HEADINGTON

I must begin with *Mont Juic*, a suite of four pieces based on Catalan dances and songs which Sir Lennox Berkeley and Lord Britten, then untitled young men at the very start of their careers, heard in Barcelona in 1936. The occasion was a contemporary music festival at which their music was played, one work each. Berkeley's was an Overture, a piece which he has since withdrawn; but what does survive from that visit is the orchestral suite which the two composers wrote in what was evidently a happy collaboration. Who exactly composed which parts of the *Mont Juic* Suite is a fairly well-kept secret, but the opening of the work bears some Berkeleian fingerprints I think. The performance on record is conducted by the composer (Berkeley, that is!) with the London Philharmonic Orchestra, together with music by Bliss, Holst, and Walton. The number is Lyrita SRCS 50.

From the particular to the general. Lyrita is a company that has been good to Berkeley's music, as indeed it has to contemporary or near-contemporary British music as a whole. Among available records featuring Berkeley's music, six Lyrita discs are wholly devoted to this one composer; and no other record company has yet done nearly as much. No matter perhaps, for the quality of playing and recording alike is so generally high on Lyrita that I am happy to praise both the music and the admirable presentation of it. A very useful orchestral collection, again from this company, has older and newer Berkeley, the Serenade and Divertimento of 1940 and 1943 together with the Partita and Canzonetta of 1965 and 1973. Although the twenty-one-year-old Decca 'Eclipse' Serenade under Münchinger is still available and worth hearing, the 1975 account under the composer's baton is more idiomatic and of course better recorded. I have fond memories of the old 78s of the Divertimento on Decca with Anthony Bernard, too, but the Lyrita performance gives more point and detail, the Scherzo being taken a little slower than one remembered, but perhaps all the more subtle for that. The Divertimento of 1943, together with the Serenade, Partita, and the brief Canzonetta for oboe and chamber orchestra, is on Lyrita SRCS 74; and it is the sort of music which led critics to recall Berkeley's French training under Nadia Boulanger and talk about his 'Gallic charm and wit' until that phrase became a misleading cliché. Those qualities are there all right, but represent only a part of Berkeley's musical personality. The lyrical English side of him perhaps comes out most obviously in his songs and choral pieces, of which there have been many. One of the earliest examples is performed by his friends Peter Pears and Benjamin Britten. Written as early as 1933, it is a setting of Herrick's 'How Love Came In' and is part of an English song recital which also includes the playing of Julian Bream in the lute songs on the second side: the number is Decca 'Eclipse' ECS 545.

Of course, the Berkeley representation on that disc is very brief: just that one song in fact. And that leads me to mention the other cliché about this composer, namely that he is a miniaturist. He himself has said that he does not as a rule feel inclined to work on a 'grand scale': works like *Belshazzar's Feast* or the *War Requiem*, huge canvases in content as well as duration, are not quite his style. But, as so often with Berkeley, that is not the whole story. There are, for instance, four symphonies to date, and concertos for piano, flute, guitar, and violin. The Piano Sonata of 1945 is also on a fairly large scale. Colin Horsley, who has so often been associated with Berkeley's piano music, has recorded the Sonata, the Six Preludes, and some shorter pieces on a 1959 Lyrita disc in mono only (Lyrita RCS 9) and despite its age the recording is still perfectly adequate.

Of Berkeley's four symphonies the first three have been recorded: no doubt the Fourth, composed in 1978, will follow in due course. The Second Symphony of 1957 represents the composer's deeper utterance, the contemplative quality which we find in some of his religious music. The big rhetorical climax in the slow movement, for example, is openly passionate in a way that is comparatively rare in Berkeley but perhaps all the more effective for that. The Second Symphony is coupled with the Piano Concerto, with David Wilde as the soloist, and these works are played by the London Philharmonic and New Philharmonia Orchestras respectively, conducted by Nicholas Braithwaite (Lyrita SRCS 94).

The Third Symphony was composed in 1969. It is in one continuous movement, closely argued and energetic, with very little thematic repetition, unity being achieved through a kind of continuous development. It is a tough but rewarding work which reminds us that the composer, though he has his lighter and more immediately charming side, also admires such intellectually powerful musicians as Roussel, Hindemith, and Frank Martin. It is on Lyrita SRCS 57, with the London Philharmonic Orchestra conducted by the composer, and the record also includes works by Maconchy, Alwyn, and Geoffrey Bush.

There are still some regrettable gaps in the Berkeley recorded catalogue. We badly need a large-scale vocal work, or more than one, of the calibre of the *Stabat Mater*, Magnificat, or the *Three Latin Motets* of 1972; and we ought to have one of the operas, the charmingly written *A Dinner Engagement* being probably the obvious choice. The Violin Concerto written for and recorded by Yehudi Menuhin is out of the catalogue and should be restored; so should the Horn Trio with Dennis Brain for whom it was composed. A recording evidently exists of the four St Teresa Songs with string orchestra, sung by the late Kathleen Ferrier, no less, to whom this beautiful work was dedicated and who gave its first performance: this was a private recording in that celebrated singer's possession, and though technically it may not meet present-day recording standards it is surely an historical document of importance which many would wish to have available.

So far, all but one of the records I have mentioned have come from Lyrita. However, the next is from another relatively small but enterprising company, Pearl. They have issued a Bridge, Bax, and Berkeley disc with the latter composer's String Trio in a clear if somewhat dry sound-style. The Trio, written in 1944 just after the orchestral Divertimento, is sinewy but far from charmless. It is played by John Georgiadis, Brian Hawkins, and Douglas Cummings on Pearl SHE 547, together with chamber music by Bax and Bridge. The Duo for Cello and Piano was composed nearly thirty later in 1971. It is a rondo-shaped piece with a four-note motto theme dominating its single movement, closely argued rather in the style of the Third Symphony which preceded it by a couple of years. Julian Lloyd Webber and John McCabe have recorded the Duo, together with music by Fricker, Dalby, and McCabe, on L'Oiseau-Lyre DSLO 18.

So far, most of these Berkeley records have been of instrumental music. In fact he has written a great number of vocal works, from solo songs and song cycles to choral pieces (some of them like the Magnificat on a large scale) and of course a full-length opera, *Nelson*, as well as shorter operas. The sacred music is important. His Missa Brevis (1960), to Latin words, written for the Westminster Cathedral Choir in which his son Michael sang, is a sustained and rich piece with organ accompaniment, and it is recorded on a disc called 'Mass at St Chad's' – that is the Catholic Cathedral Church of Birmingham; however it is split up liturgically with the other items of the Mass so that one cannot really play it straight through. The record is directed by John Harper with his St Chad's Choir, and it is on Abbey LPB 768. Another Abbey issue, this time recorded in Chichester Cathedral, has a rather higher technical quality, and is an Anglican piece composed in 1975 for the composer's old friend Walter Hussey, a great patron of the arts and Dean of Chichester Cathedral. It is a setting of Psalm 23, 'The Lord is my Shepherd', and begins with a characteristically unforced treble solo sung by Andrew Wicks. The performance is directed by John Birch with the Chichester Cathedral Choir and the number is Abbey LPB 770.

Among other Berkeley issues I must mention are the Lyrita disc of the First Symphony and Two-Piano Concerto, Peter and Meriel Dickinson's song recital on Argo ZRG 788 including the Chinese Songs which are among the composer's own favourites, and the Peter Pears performance on Decca Headline of the Four Ronsard Sonnets. There is also a Meridian record, which includes the Piano and Wind Quintet of 1975, as well as some piano music and songs (E. 77017); and I look forward to the Unicorn recording of the Antiphon for string orchestra which is to be released with Michael Berkeley's *Meditations*. Finally, I find myself tempted to call attention to an early work, the Flute Sonatina of 1939, which has appeared in a sparkling performance by the 'Man with the Golden Flute' – so says the record sleeve anyway – James Galway, with the pianist Anthony Goldstone. It comes from RCA on LRL1 5127.

Recordings of Works Discussed

Canzonetta. London Philharmonic Orchestra/Berkeley	Lyrita SRCS 74
Chinese Songs. M. Dickinson/P. Dickinson	Argo ZRG 788
Concerto for Piano and Orchestra Op.29. Wilde/New Philharmonia Orchestra/Braithwaite	Lyrita SRCS 94
Concerto for Two Pianos and Orchestra Op.30. Beckett/McDonald/London Philharmonic Orchestra/Del Mar	Lyrita SRCS 80
Divertimento in B flat. London Philharmonic Orchestra/Berkeley	Lyrita SRCS 74
Duo for Cello and Piano. Lloyd-Webber/McCabe	Oiseau-Lyre DSLO 18
Four Piano Pieces Op.32. Horsley (1 and 2 only)	Lyrita RCS 9
Four Ronsard Sonnets. Pears/London Sinfonietta/Berkeley	Decca HEAD 3
'How Love Came in'. Pears/Britten	Decca ECS 545
Missa Brevis. Choir of St Chad's Cathedral, Birmingham/Harper	Abbey LPB 768
Mont Juic Op.9. London Philharmonic Orchestra/Berkeley	Lyrita SRCS 50
Partita for Chamber Orchestra. London Philharmonic Orchestra/Berkeley	Lyrita SRCS 74
Quintet for Piano and Wind Op. 90. Stuttgart Chamber Orchestra/Münchinger.	Meridian E77017
Serenade for Strings Op.12. Stuttgart Chamber Orchestra/Münchinger.	Decca ECS 688
Serenade for Strings Op.12. London Philharmonic Orchestra/Berkeley	Lyrita SRCS 74
Six Piano Preludes Op.23. Horsley	Lyrita SRCS 94
Sonata for Piano Op.20. Horsley	Lyrita SRCS 94
String Trio Op.19. Georgiadis/Hawkins/Cummings	Pearl SHE 547
Sonatina for Flute and Piano Op.13. Galway/Goldstone	RCA LRL 1 5127
Symphony No. 1 Op.16. London Philharmonic Orchestra/Del Mar	Lyrita SRCS 80
Symphony No.2. Op.51. London Philharmonic Orchestra/Braithwaite	Lyrita SRCS 94
Symphony No.3. London Philharmonic Orchestra/Berkeley	Lyrita SRCS 57
'The Lord is my Shepherd'. Chichester Cathedral Choir/Birch	Abbey LPB 770

© Christopher Headington

Introduction to Frank Bridge

ANTHONY PAYNE

As recently as five or six years ago a survey of Bridge's music on record would have been unthinkable, as there were only two major works on disc. This reflected a widespread ignorance of his music and lamentably helped to perpetuate it. In fact Bridge was the last to be rehabilitated amongst a whole group of composers of Vaughan Williams's generation, which became neglected in the 1940s and '50s. By 1973, for instance, Bax, Moeran, and Ireland had all been well served on LP, while Bridge still languished in obscurity. Yet Bridge was the most stylistically interesting of his generation, and the least deserving of neglect on grounds of quality of vision and craftsmanship.

I mentioned 1973 because we can ascribe quite positively to this year a revival in Bridge's fortunes: it was the year in which Argo issued their splendid recording of the Third and Fourth String Quartets in conjunction with the British Council. This powerful and compelling music must have come as quite a shock to the generations of music lovers who had grown up since the war, and missed the one or two isolated broadcasts and performances of his music during that time. We might well ask how such music could have taken so long to reach us through the gramophone. Both quartets are outstandingly well played by the Allegri String Quartet, and I cannot imagine a finer introduction to Bridge's mature style than this particular disc. The Third and Fourth Quartets are issued by Argo (ZRG 714).

During the course of this survey I shall be indicating how much of the late music is sad and sombre in tone, and often intensely private. But the sadness does not have an easy passage, for Bridge's character was far from passive. Towards the end of his life, in works like the Fourth Quartet, Bridge turned to a more Classical and concentrated manner, like Bartók, Schoenberg, and Szymanowski at comparable stages in their careers. His iron control over emotionally ambivalent forces is celebrated in passages of hard-won optimism. This is the music of a man of deep spiritual courage, and one of the most radically original composers England has produced. Bridge's output was dominated by chamber music, and enough of it has been recorded now for us to trace in it the whole of the composer's truly remarkable development of style: few composers have charted such an extraordinary course from deeply conservative beginnings to radical final years, but for those who are still hazy about Bridge (and there is precious little literature about him even now), I ought perhaps to mention the background facts. He was born in 1879 and died in 1941, and unlike many of his fellow Stanford pupils he seemed content with the somewhat Brahmsian training he had received. A Germanic musical discourse, tinged with Gallic grace and precision served Bridge throughout his early years. The music he wrote at this time was tailored to a rather conservative public, and for this reason it can sound a little faded to us today, but by the time of the First World War his music was becoming increasingly chromatic, and it was inclining towards the sort of Englishness he had so far avoided. For instance there are points of resemblance to Delius, Ireland, and even Butterworth.

The really startling developments, though, were still to come. Benjamin Britten, who was Bridge's most distinguished pupil, has told us about his teacher's passionate pacifist convictions, and the catastrophe of the Great War seems to have released a vein in Bridge which had previously remained untapped. The tradition which had fostered his early work had quite literally been blown asunder along with countless lives and hopes. The void clearly had to be filled, and by a new manner. The tone was to be one of passionate protest, restless energy, and elegiac half-lights, and it was to be coloured by Bridge's recently acquired sympathy with avant-garde composers of the time like Berg, Skryabin, and Bartók. Such was the music of the Third Quartet and of most of his subsequent pieces. It could only have been the result of a most disturbing upheaval in Bridge's personality.

The contrast between this new style and the easy-going, conservative Edwardian Bridge is encapsulated for us on yet another Argo disc, this time featuring the Tunnell Trio. Joined by the violinist Brian Hawkins they play the finest of the early chamber pieces, the Phantasy Piano Quartet. This is music of touching romantic innocence and it is characteristically of a typically fastidious craftsmanship. But the glory of this record is the Tunnell Trio's magisterial performance of the Second Piano Trio, one of the master-pieces of twentieth-century English, indeed European, chamber music. The compositional mastery is demonstrable at every turn, but how are we to describe its unique sound and poetry. It is passionate, yet detached, fiercely triumphant at the close, yet unable to avoid a final coda of the most poignant withdrawal. It is a work of monumental grandeur which goes far beyond any words we may apply to it. The record number is Argo ZK 40.

Next I must mention a Pearl record which is mostly given over to music by Bax and Berkeley but which includes one of Bridge's most remarkable chamber works, the Trio (Rhapsody) for the unusual combination of two violins and viola. This strangely elusive piece sometimes bitingly incisive, sometimes fugitive and melancholy is excellently played by John Georgiadis, Neil Watson, and Brian Hawkins on SHE 547.

Before leaving the world of Bridge's chamber music I would like to mention one of the few recorded performances which was available before Argo's pioneering issue of the string quartets. This is Rostropovich's and

Britten's magnificent interpretation of the Cello Sonata. This powerful work dates from the composer's middle period, and so it completes the picture of his stylistic progress. The sonata is more concentrated and chromatic in manner than, say, the Phantasy Piano Quartet; but it leaves little or no indication of the final radical manner. It receives a superb performance, full of passion and warmth yet tightly controlled; and it leaves us with sad memories of Britten's matchless keyboard powers. It comes from Decca on SXL 6426 and is coupled with Schubert's 'Arpeggione' Sonata. I must add that there is another performance of the Cello Sonata, a fine one by Rohan and Duvi de Saram, which at the moment provides the only, major, alternative choice of interpretation in the Bridge discography. What is more it is coupled with the violin sonata, a splendid example of late-Bridge which is finely played by Levon Chilingirian and Clifford Benson. This issues does leave a little to be desired in terms of recorded sound but is still recommended. The number is Pearl SHE 541.

I have already referred to the great change that came over Bridge's music in the mid-1920s, and that the catastrophe of the 1914–18 war may have triggered it. The work that first embodied the new sounds, the Piano Sonata, was significantly dedicated to a young composer killed in France. This is obviously a key work in understanding Bridge's artistic growth, and it is a little sad that a recording on Pearl has already had to be deleted. It also includes a representative collection of songs, but some songs can be heard on a Pears/Britten recital album, including a totally authentic performance of ''Tis but a week'. The records come from Decca, and the numbers are ZK 28–9.

Turning now to Bridge's orchestral music there is a recording by Sir Charles Groves and the Royal Liverpool Philharmonic Orchestra which includes some of his finest works in each of his three creative periods. For many years the only orchestral piece by Bridge most people knew was his symphonic suite *The Sea*. It is an earlyish work composed in 1910, and we know that the composer came to resent its popularity as against his later and much greater music. Nevertheless Sir Charles Groves and his players confirm the music's vitality. And if we do not expect too much of it, the heart can still lift to its simple romanticism. Yet however well you may respond to *The Sea*, I think there is no doubting the superiority of the short tone poem *Summer*. This little gem was completed in 1915 and shows the richly English vein the composer adopted in his middle creative years. There is a fine elevation in this piece that floods our sensibilities. The chief attraction on this representative disc of Bridge's orchestral music, however, is once more to be found in the latest work, the rhapsody *Enter Spring* which was composed in 1927. It is unique in being the only untroubled and exuberant work of Bridge's later years, a time which was almost totally given over to restless, melancholy music. This piece seems to have been completely neglected after its first performance at the 1927 Norwich Festival, and when I heard Benjamin Britten's splendid revival of it in the late 1960s I remember feeling aghast that such music of such energy and breadth could have become forgotten. I think Sir Charles Groves adopts a slightly pedestrian tempo for the opening section, but that is my only reservation concerning both interpretation and playing on this record. Certainly the treatment of the work's middle section is exemplary, and what magic is distilled at this point in the music. For the only time in his maturity, Bridge returns here to the tradition of English mature music and it produces sounds that still the heart (HMV ASD 3190).

There is a further orchestral disc devoted to short English pieces in performances by Neville Dilkes and the English Sinfonia. Only one work by Bridge is included, but it is a masterpiece, and that makes the record a must for anybody interested in the composer. The piece is called *There is a Willow Grows Aslant a Brook*, and it inhabits that world of twilight and mourning so typical of the composer's maturity. Mr Dilkes and his players do a fine job on what is one Bridge's most individual and concentrated scores, a miracle of resourcefulness and poetry in its use of small orchestra (HMV CSD 3696). Another record of considerable importance, although only partly devoted to Bridge gives us the piano concertante work *Phantasm*, very well performed by Peter Wallfisch with the London Philharmonic Orchestra under Nicholas Braithwaite. This is a strange work, inhabiting a world of what we might tentatively call English expressionism. It is not an unflawed piece, and some of the more improvisatory solo writing seems a little perfunctory, but long stretches of the music sustain an eerie dreamscope of extraordinary originality and intensity. *Phantasm* is coupled with Moeran's Third Rhapsody, on Lyrita SRCS 91.

Bridge left us a comparatively small legacy of orchestral music, and produced only five works during his final phase. Three of these have now been recorded and issued, and I have mentioned each of them. The other two, though, have also been recorded and I hope will be released soon: one of the works, the cello concerto called *Oration*, is Bridge's orchestral masterpiece, and one of the greatest of all twentieth-century concerted works. I know my claims for it may seem high, but I have long been convinced of its stature and I urge music lovers of all persuasions to pounce the moment it is issued.

Finally I must include two records of string music, one chamber and one orchestral. I have left them until last because they deal almost exclusively with the early Bridge and I think they should be treated as filling out the picture established by later and more impressive works. The first is a record of early quartet pieces very well characterized by the Gabrieli String Quartet. It consists of the Novelletten and the Idylls. The second Idyll you will remember furnished Britten with the theme for his famous Variations on a Theme of Frank Bridge. The number is Decca SDD 497. The record string orchestral music comes from Lyrita, and includes the string arrangements *Sir Roger de Coverley*, *Cherry Ripe*, and *Sally in our Alley*. These are charming trifles, but it is chiefly to be recommended for the deeply felt *Lament* and the Suite for Strings, one of the finest of Bridge's early works. The performances, by the London Philharmonic Orchestra under Sir Adrian Boult, are sympathetic. (SRCS 73).

All in all the situation with Bridge recordings is not too bad, even if we may regret the lack of alternative versions of certain key works. Five years ago practically nothing was available, now only a few of the most important works need recording, the Second String Quartet being perhaps the most urgent. This being so I could perhaps sum up and say that four of the records I have mentioned will give a fine representative impression of Bridge's still very much underestimated and unfamiliar art. The Third and Fourth Quartets; the Phantasy Piano Quartet and Second Piano Trio, the record of orchestral music including *The Sea, Summer*, and *Enter Spring*; and the forthcoming record of *Oration*, which will also include the lovely middle-period piece *Two Poems* and Bridge's last work the overture *Rebus*.

Recordings of Works Discussed

Cherry Ripe, for string orchestra. London Philharmonic Orchestra/Boult	Lyrita SRCS 73
Enter Spring, rhapsody. Royal Liverpool Philharmonic Orchestra/Groves	HMV ASD 3190
Lament, for string orchestra. London Philharmonic Orchestra/Boult	Lyrita SRCS 73
Phantasm, rhapsody for piano and orchestra. Wallfisch/London Philharmonic Orchestra/Braithwaite	Lyrita SRCS 91
Phantasy Piano Quartet. Tunnel Trio/Hawkins	Argo ZK 40
Piano Trio No.2. Tunnell Trio	Argo ZK 40
Sally in our Alley. London Philharmonic Orchestra/Boult	Lyrita SRCS 73
Sir Roger de Coverley, Christmas dance for string orchestra. London Philharmonic Orchestra/Boult	Lyrita SRCS 73
Sonata for Cello and Piano. Rostropovich/Britten	Decca SXL 6426
Sonata for Cello and Piano. R. de Saram/D. de Saram	Pearl SHE 541
Sonata for Violin and Piano. Chilingirian/Benson	Pearl SHE 541
String Quartet no.3. Allegri Quartet	Argo ZRG 714
String Quartet no.4. Allegri Quartet	Argo ZRG 714
Suite for String Orchestra. London Philharmonic Orchestra/Boult	Lyrita SRCS 73
Summer, tone poem. Royal Liverpool Philharmonic Orchestra/Groves	HMV ASD 3190
The Sea, symphonic suite. Royal Liverpool Philharmonic Orchestra/Groves	HMV ASD 3190
There is a Willow Grows Aslant a Brook, for small orchestra. English Sinfonia/Dilkes	HMV CSD 3696

Three Idylls. Gabrieli Quartet	Decca SDD 497
Three Novelletten – Gabrieli Quartet	Decca SDD 497
''Tis but a Week'. Pears/Britten	Decca ZK 28–9
Trio (rhapsody) for two violins and viola. Georgiadis/ Watson/Hawkins	Pearl SHE 547

Note: Since I made this survey, the Bridge discography has continued to grow, and two recent issues can be whole-heartedly welcomed. A superbly performed and recorded interpretation of the Piano Sonata by Eric Parkin, together with a sequence of short pieces (Unicorn RHS 359), fills the serious gap which I have lamented (p.154); and an equally fine disc by the Music Group of London containing the Phantasie Piano Trio and Piano Quintet very nearly completes the picture of early Bridge (Enigma K 53578). Valuable additions, both, though they do not affect my choice of four representative records.

© Anthony Payne